THE WISH BOOKLET
Volume X

Wardrobe for a Little Girl 1900 — 1910

By Susan Bonsall Sirkis

ISBN 0-913786-10-1
3rd Reprinting

This is my favorite little German bisque doll. Just ten inches tall, she is marked 1079-2 DEP SH. Some of her new clothes form a background.

THE WISH BOOKLET

Seven years ago, I had an idea which culminated in the first Wish Booklet. It was just a little idea, but it grew and it continues to grow. As that idea strives each year for increased maturity, I myself grow richer in the benefits of friends met and ideas shared. This is the time I would like to say an especial thank you to all the dolls who make wishing possible and the people who imbue in those lovely little dolls the spirit of recall.

A few years ago there were scant resources for doll dressmakers. Mary Julian Glover and Alberta Anderson were two who made patterns for doll dressmakers. Otherwise, patterns were often cherished (and often tattered) bits of tissue passed from friend to friend. When they were sold, they were sometimes rough and not quite workable. There were not enough contributions to publications like the Toy Trader and Doll News. Now there are many privately printed patterns and booklets of patterns available. The doll dressmaker can pick and choose. Evelyn Ackerman, E. J. Carter, Atha Kahler, Barbara Jendrick and Barbara Bannister, to name a few, have produced contributions to the doll pattern library. Many of the available period patterns are reprints of contemporary material. Some are original. Both have their place on our shelves. Not too much dependence, however, should be placed on doll patterns. Each and every doll is different. Even two rag dolls made by the same person from the same pattern on the same day will be different. The very best patterns therefore, the ones that fit, are made for *that* specific doll. The sooner you can learn to use commercial patterns as a guide to the *shape* of the patterns you cut, the better your doll's clothes will fit.

The decade from 1900 - 1910 was the era of the German bisque doll. Most of the beautiful German dolls were made then, and most were exported to other countries like America. The charming innocent period prior to World War I had peace and quiet - time for mama to make wonderful wardrobes for daughter's dolls and then time for mother to teach daughter how to make clothes for the same prized doll (and incidently teaching her good sewing techniques which would last a lifetime).

For the purposes of this booklet, I have narrowed the time element down still further - the years 1904 through 1909 have provided me with all the material used to formulate the wardrobe. Styles were not simple; innocent perhaps, but not simple. The application of insertion and lace had diminished only slightly from the previous decade. Adult women's garments required just as much engineering underneath the simple flowing silhouette as before. The emphasis had merely been shifted from overpowering femininity to overwhelming charm.

This change was also reflected in little girls' clothes. They (the little girls) found themselves between restriction and liberation. Ten years before, they wore large sleeves and longer skirts. Hair was invariably worn long and shoes were *very* dainty - altogether an uncomfortable situation for a small girl. In ten more years she would be wearing rompers to play in the mud. Just now however, in the early years of the century, little girls were in between. Their clothing required lining and a great deal of trim, although their skirts were shorter. Lingerie, however, was an exception. It had already lost its earlier lacy handmade look and had begun to assume a utilitarian unromantic aspect.

It is not my practice to present drawings in the Wish Booklets unless there is a separate pattern for the garment. Therefore, I have not drawn each of the many variations possible for any of the dresses. The length of the sleeves may be shortened or lengthened, necklines raised or lowered, lace ruffles added or omitted, or skirts pleated or gathered. The patterns in this booklet may be, and should be mixed and matched. Change sleeves, switch bodices, vary skirt treatments to achieve an infinite variety of dresses.

You will notice that the directions for most of the dresses mention linings. A pattern for the linings is given. Linings are so important for this period. Take the time to make them for each dress. Linings may be either white batiste or self-material if not too bulky. Be sure to press each seam as you go. Try spray fabric finish on cottons. It doesn't stiffen like spray starch.

I am repeating the pattern and instructions for the rag doll which appeared in Volume IX, however the clothes in this booklet were drafted for a 10" bisque-head, jointed-body doll of the period. The garments also fit the rag doll.

The demands of space require that I scramble the patterns somewhat. Please make sure that you have all the patterns for each garment before you begin to lay out.

Most of the German bisque dolls are somewhat larger than my petite child. There are three methods of enlarging the patterns. One is the "square" method, very well described in each issue of McCall's Needlework and Crafts. The second method involves the use of the pantograph, available at most good art or office supply shops. The third, and best, is the method of folding, cutting and snipping - in short, making your own pattern by cutting muslin to fit your own doll.

I wish you all knew my husband Mike, and my good friend Helen, who make these booklets more Booklet than Wish!

Reston, Virginia
November 1972

Susan Sirkis

THE DOLL

The first important thing that you should learn about doll making is that you must always sign and date your dolls. There are many reasons for this, not the least of which is that you will want to watch your own progress in the art. Who knows, in time, you may become so well known as a doll maker that a special doll will be prized by collectors a bit more because it bears your signature.

While mass production techniques can be used to make these dolls, I prefer to make them either individually or in pairs. This method I find, insures that each doll has its separate and complete personality. It is easy to impart personality to these dolls. All it needs is a little flick of the wrist when you are painting the face. A smile, a frown, a wink and freckles are all variants that can be introduced.

The doll can be increased in size by eliminating the stitching line and sewing on the cutting line. This adds a full inch to the height of the doll. It works the other way too - sew inside the stitching line to make the doll smaller. DO NOT forget to alter the clothes patterns.

The dolls can be made straight legged by cutting the legs and torso together. Just pin the legs to the bottom of the torso before cutting. Be sure to eliminate both seam allowances or you will find your doll growing the way most children do - unexpectedly.

Cloth dolls can be made of unbleached muslin and stuffed with cotton or polyester. Flesh colored cotton or felt may also be used but avoid too pinky a tone as this will make the doll look as if it is suffering from scarlet fever.

If you are sewing by hand, use a back-stitch. If you are sewing on a machine, use a narrow zig-zag-stitch and go over that with a short straight stitch. The more trustworthy these seams are, the more firmly you will be able to stuff your doll. Carefully stitch all seams. Trim material close to stitching. Clip all curves. Turn. Stuff firmly. Make darts in feet after legs are partially stuffed. In other words, stuff the feet a little bit past the point where the bend should occur. Bend the foot up and sew in place. If you painted the face on before you stuffed the doll, make sure the feet are in the same direction as the face. Fold under raw edges at top of arms and legs. Sew together. Sew arms and legs to torso. Put 2" of narrow dowel in the neck and stuff around it. Finish stuffing head and pin closed. Wrap a strip of muslin about ½" wide tightly around neck and smooth top and face by gently pulling and tugging.

For some of the hairdos, it will be necessary for the dolls to have ears. Sew the ears together. Trim very close to the seam. Clip and turn. Run a gathering thread along straight raw edge and pull up just slightly. Turn raw edge under and whip to side seam on a level with the eyes and nose. Make one stitch in center of ear. See sketch.

Features may be embroidered or drawn on with indelible felt tip drawing pens. Use the sketches in the booklet for ideas to develop your own doll's features. Use the full sized sample as a guide. Don't forget to give some of the children freckles - tiny dots of brown felt tip pen, not too many though. A red pencil lightly rubbed across the cheeks will impart a radiant glow of health.

Hair can be made of yarn, embroidery floss, mohair, or synthetic hair from a dime store hair piece. Arrange hair as shown in individual sketches. Sew hair directly to the head with thread that matches the hair. Curls can be made like big French knots when yarn or floss is used. They can also be made by dampening the hair and wrapping it around large metal knitting needles.

Legs can be made of black, grey or white material to represent stockings. When socks are indicated, legs can be cut off at the proper place and feet can be replaced with sock colored fabric. To do this, sew the two fabrics together and press seam; then place pattern on fabric with the marker. This is especially effective when striped stockings are required.

Make stands for straight legged dolls by cutting a tiny hole in the back of each foot above the shoe. Run swab stick all the way up back of leg under muslin "skin". Insert end of swabs into blocks of wood with holes drilled to receive them. The bases may be covered with paper or fabric or they may be sanded and stained. If the doll is wearing socks or stockings, you will have to cut a tiny hole in them also.

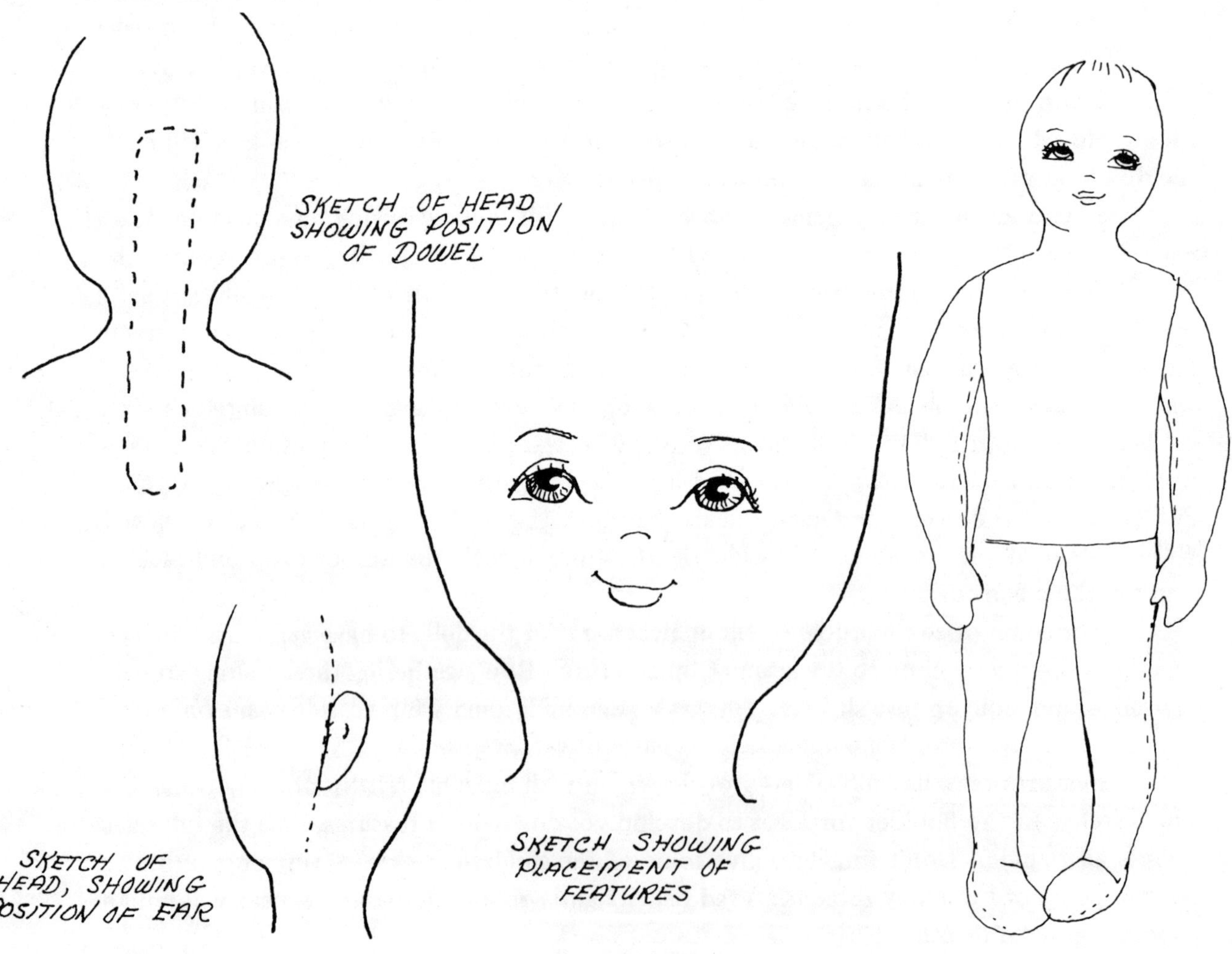

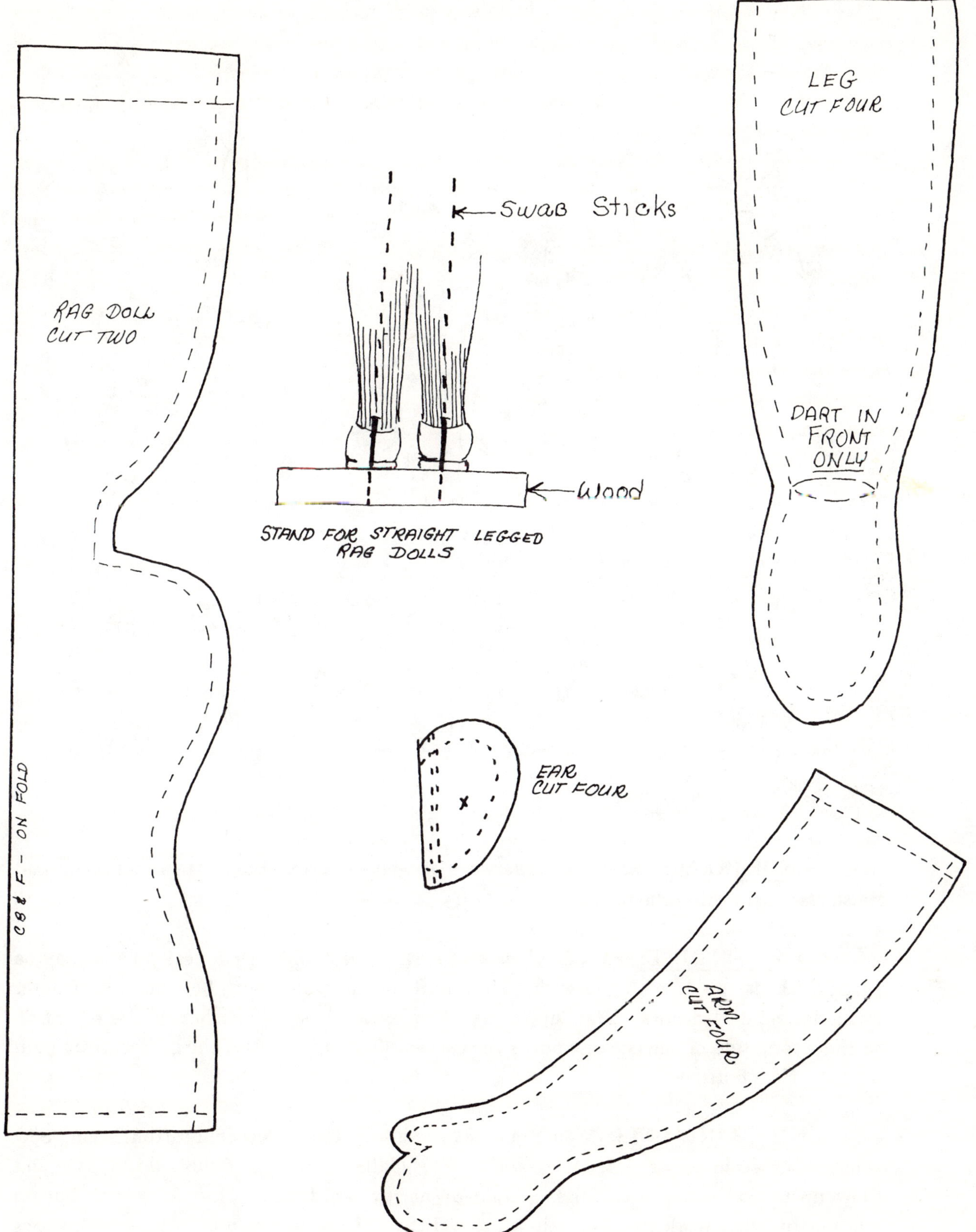
RAG DOLL
CUT TWO
CB & F - ON FOLD
Swab Sticks
Wood
STAND FOR STRAIGHT LEGGED
RAG DOLLS
LEG
CUT FOUR
DART IN
FRONT
ONLY
EAR
CUT FOUR
ARM
CUT FOUR

THE CLOTHES

UNDERWEAR: Make the underwear of white batiste. French seam all seams and finish raw edges with rolled hems.

1 - CHEMISE: Sew shoulder seams. Hem armholes. Hem neck. These may be edged with narrow lace if you wish. Hem back opening and work buttonholes. Gather along double dotted lines. Draw up so that chemise fits waist. Whip short pieces of ribbon to the wrong side of the chemise under the gathers. This will prevent the gathers from pulling out. Hem bottom.

2 - PANTALETS: Make pin tucks along solid lines. Sew center front seam. Sew center back seam below dot. Hem above dot. Gather top along double dotted line and draw up to fit waist over chemise. Mount on narrow waistband. Close back with button and buttonhole. Work two buttonholes in waistband front and two in back. Sew buttons to chemise. Sew leg seams. Hem bottoms and trim with narrow lace.

3 - PETTICOAT: Cut a piece of fabric 20" by 4". Make a ½" hem in bottom and trim with narrow lace. Work three pin tucks above hem. Use the pantalets pattern as a guide. Close center back seam, leaving 1½" open for placket. Hem placket. Gather petticoat to a waistband. Close waistband with button and buttonhole.

4 - STOCKINGS: Make the stockings from the tops of baby socks. Buy white ones and leave them white or dye them black. To match either the dress or the ribbon trim on white dresses, buy pastel socks. Place top of pattern at top of baby sock. For doll socks, rather than stockings, place dotted line on pattern at top of baby sock. Sew center back seam. Place on doll's foot. The stocking will mold to the doll's foot in a few days.

5 - PAJAMAS: Make the pajamas of flannel in white or pastel color. Sew shoulder seams. Hem back opening. Face back edges of pajamas to the solid line. Gather top and sew to bottom of yoke. Narrowly bind neck and trim with lace. Hem bottom of trousers. Sew sleeve seams. Gather tops of sleeves and sew sleeves to pajamas. Gather bottoms of sleeves and mount on narrow cuffs. Edge cuffs with lace.

6 - ROBE: Make the robe of printed flannel, lined with solid flannel. Sew shoulder seams. Gather top of skirt and sew to bottom of yoke. Sew center seam on collar. Sew collar to back of yoke. Sew sleeve seam. Gather sleeve tops and set sleeves in armscyes. Make the lining and the outer part separately. Then join by placing right sides together and sewing along front edges and around collar. Turn. Slip-stitch bottom of sleeves and skirt to the lining.

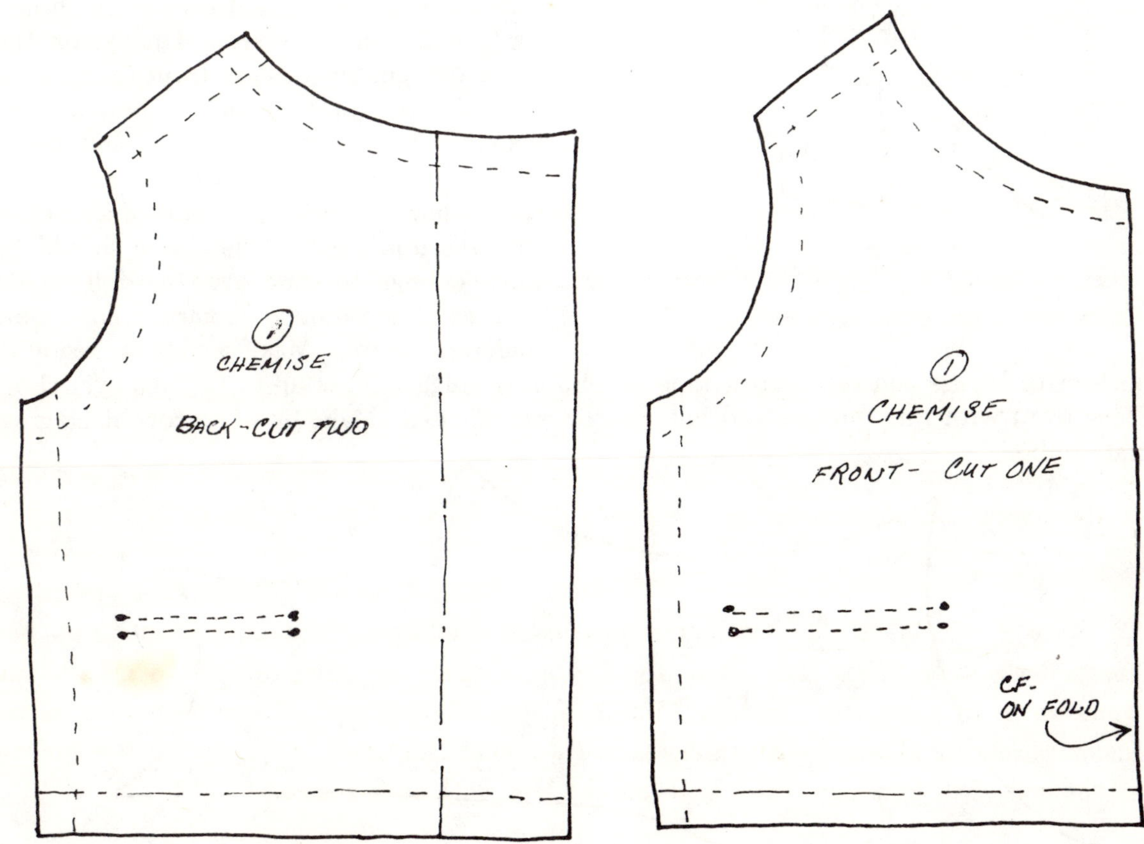

7 - MIDDY BLOUSE & SKIRT:

The middy blouse and skirt are made of harmonizing fabrics, one plain and one checked or plaid. The collar of the blouse, the cuffs and the skirt should match. The underbodice, attached to the skirt, is made of white batiste with a narrow stand-up collar and insert which matches the skirt. The doll should wear black stockings and boots.

UNDERBODICE & SKIRT: Turn under seam allowance of insert and baste in place to front of underbodice. Sew shoulder seams of underbodice. Turn under back edges and hem. Make narrow stand-up collar. Hem armscyes. Sew underarm seams. Cut the skirt 24" x 4". Make a ½" hem. Pleat in center front to fit bottom of underbodice. Sew center back seam. Close back with four snaps.

BLOUSE: Sew shoulder seams. Sew collar sections together, right sides facing. Clip seams, turn and press. Trim outside edge with narrow black braid. Baste collar in place around neck, on the outer or right side. Turn front facing back over the top of the collar. Sew around neck. Turn facing to inside and press. Gather tops of sleeves to fit armscyes and sew in place. Gather bottoms of sleeves to fit over doll's hand (the sleeve should be loose enough to slide over the doll's hand with ease) and mount on narrow cuff. Sew underarm seam. Make a narrow casing in bottom of blouse and run narrow tape or ribbon through. Draw up to fit hips over skirt. Close front with tiny buttons and buttonholes as indicated. Make tie of narrow black grosgrain ribbon.

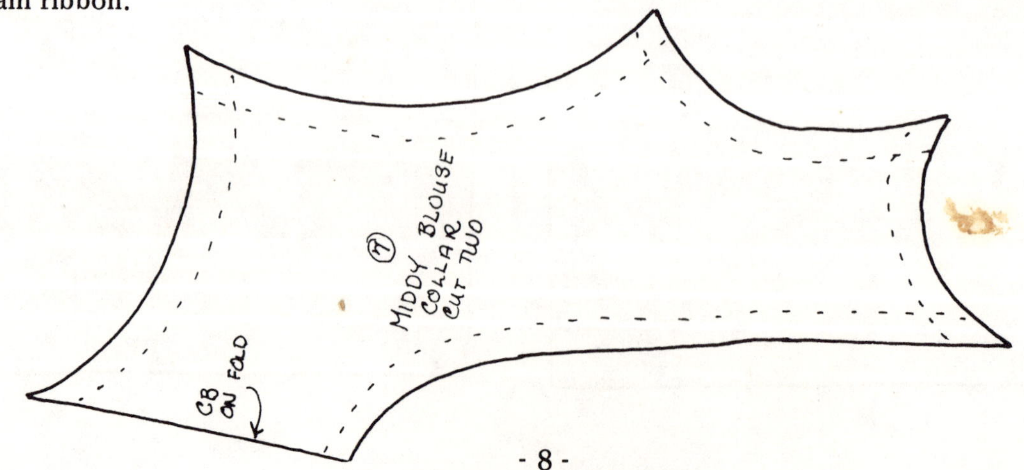

<u># 8 - YELLOW PRINT DRESS:</u> Make the dress of a floral print. Black boots or shoes should be worn. Gather bodice front along double dotted lines at neck and waist. Draw up to fit bodice front lining. Baste edges of lining pieces together. Sew shoulder seams. Sew right sides of collar pieces together. Clip seam. Turn and press. Sew the collar to the bodice, covering raw edge with narrow ribbon or bias strip of self-material. Gather sleeve tops and sew to armscyes. Gather sleeve bottoms and mount on narrow cuff. Sew underarm seams. Cut the skirt 4" x 25". Gather and sew to bottom of bodice. Sew center back seam of skirt, leaving 1¼" open for placket. Turn bodice facing under and hem. Close back with four small buttons and buttonholes. Make a ¾" hem in skirt. Make a narrow belt of self-material to button in the back. Trim as shown in drawing with rows of cable-stitch (see sketch) or narrow braid.

Trims may sometimes be much more effectively embroidered than applied. Though ready-made trims are difficult to find in a scale small enough to be of value, there are a variety of embroidery stitches which may be used or adapted. Study a good needlework book for ideas.

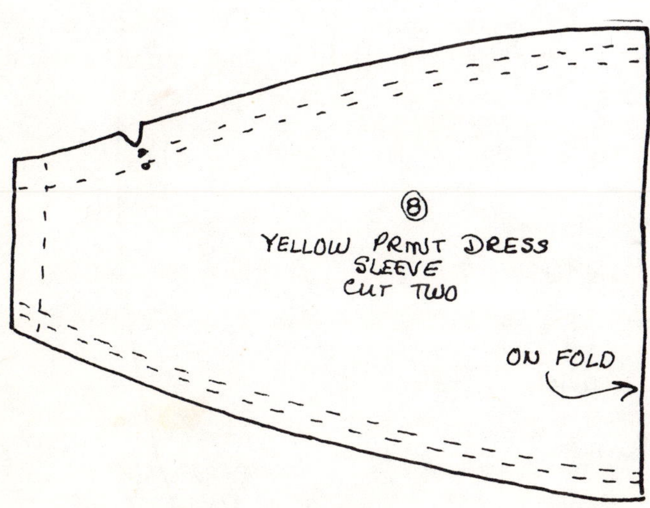

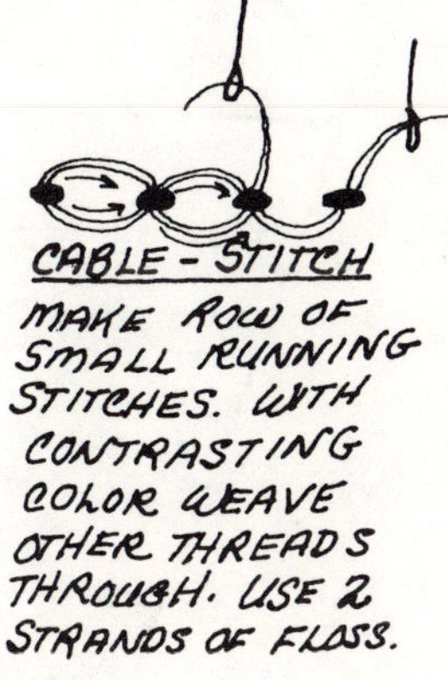

9 - PALE BLUE BATISTE DRESS:

This dress can be made either in a pale color or white. The collar, cuffs and embroidery should be white. The collar and cuffs are made either of eyelet edging or lace. The sash is a silk ribbon 1" wide and long enough to tie in a large bow in the back. Black boots and stockings or white socks and black shoes may be worn. Work the embroidery on the bodice front. Make pintucks. Gather the bottom of the bodice front and draw up to fit bottom of lining. Baste lining pieces to bodice pieces. Sew shoulder seams. Narrowly bind neck with silk ribbon or narrow bias strip. Make a collar of ½" eyelet edging and sew over the binding. Gather the tops of the sleeves and mount on eyelet cuffs. Sew underarm seams. Cut the skirt 25" x 4". Gather top to fit bottom of bodice and sew together. Hem back opening and work four buttonholes for four small buttons. Make a ½" hem in bottom of skirt.

This was a very popular style. Many photographs of little girls show the starched and painstakingly ironed white batiste dress trimmed with tucks and a wide sash.

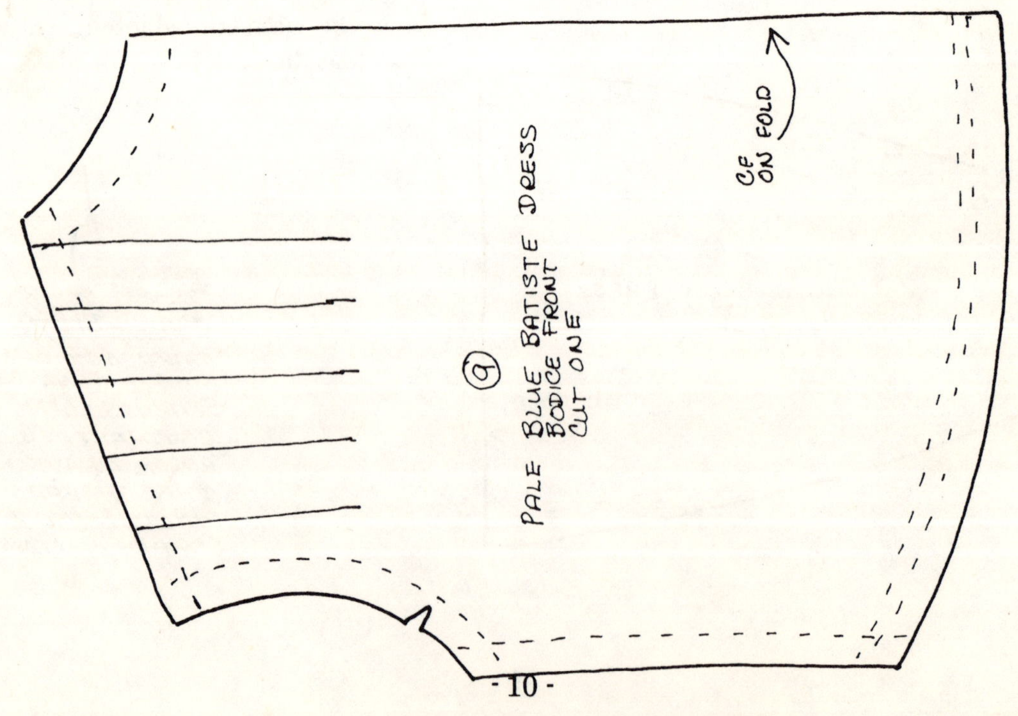

10 - PINK DRESS WITH EYELET TRIM AND BONNET: This dress should be made of pale pink batiste. It may also be made of white batiste. If you make it of white, make the sash, the ribbon in the bonnet and the shoes and stockings of a pastel color. Gather the top of the bodice front and sew to yoke. Gather the bottom of the bodice front to fit the bottom of the yoke. Baste the lining pieces and the bodice pieces together. Sew shoulder seams. Make a narrow stand-up collar of self-material. Gather tops of sleeves to fit armscyes. Mount on cuff and edge with a ½" lace ruffle. Sew underarm seams. Cut two pieces of 1" eyelet edging 4½" long and two 3½" pieces. Hem all ends. Sew two pieces together for each shoulder and edge with lace as shown. Tack in place to bodice. Make the skirt 24" x 4". Gather top to fit bottom of bodice. Gather a piece of eyelet 24" x 3". Baste skirt and eyelet together and sew to bottom of waistband. Hem back facing and sew center back seams. Make a ¾" hem in bottom of pink skirt. Close back with buttons and buttonholes. Tie a 1½" wide sash around the waist with a large bow in the back. Make the bonnet of 3" eyelet edging. Cut it 20" long. Seam the two ends together. Gather the top edge into a tight circle. Run gathering thread around the bonnet 1½" above the lower edge and draw up to fit doll's head. Tie a bow of ribbon around the bonnet. Tack in place.

In the early years of the century young girls were advised to learn how to freshen and retrim bonnets to earn extra money. The girls had to call upon their customers to discover their wishes and collect the bonnet. When the work was finished (and this must be done promptly) it was to be placed in tissue in a neat box. A note of thanks for the order was to be enclosed. For this service, girls were advised to charge 50¢.

11 - APRON: In the days when laundry was washed in iron tubs in the back yard on Monday and ironed in a hot kitchen with sad irons on Tuesday, every little girl had a good supply of aprons. Some, plain, were worn for play. Others, trimmed with lace and eyelet, were used for dressier occasions. This one may be made of white batiste and trimmed with either eyelet or lace. It may also be left plain. Make the bows of narrow silk ribbon if you trim the apron with lace, and of self-material if you do not. The dressy apron may also be made of dotted swiss. Make pleats in front, turning them in the directions shown in the sketch. Face or hem the back edges. Hem the bottom edge and trim with lace ruffle and a row of insertion as shown in sketch. Gather the two sides of back and draw up to fit doll *over* clothes. Narrowly bind top edge, including the armholes. Conceal binding under a row of insertion. Do not put insertion over binding on armholes and do not use it at all if the apron is to be plain. Sew four pieces of ¼" ribbon long enough to tie on shoulders at X's. Close back with one button and buttonhole at top.

Sooner or later, each doll dressmaker must make the decision of whether or not to dress the antique doll as a completely authentic antique - using original materials, notions and sewing techniques - or to use modern materials and techniques to produce a simulation of the original garment. The danger in the former method lies in the fact that all too frequently the redressed doll is sold as all original. The frustration inherent in this method results when old material, well preserved when stored, begins to crumble and split when exposed to air. There is a middle road between shiny new and falling apart (however attractive) old. Choose soft aged looking colors, slightly faded prints and cream lace. The affect is compatible with the doll but no question can be raised about whether or not the doll has been redressed.

<u># 12 - NAVY BLUE SKIRT AND GREEN PLAID BLOUSE:</u> This is one of the most charming outfits made for this booklet. I made it of navy blue poplin and a green and blue plaid cotton. The suspenders are trimmed with moss green braid and buttons. The skirt is faced with plaid. The doll should wear black boots and stockings. Sew the shoulder seams of the blouse. Gather neck to fit doll's neck. Turn under back facing. Make a narrow stand-up collar. Gather tops of sleeves and sew to armscyes. Gather bottom of sleeves to fit doll's wrists. Make narrow cuffs. Sew underarm seams. On inside of blouse, following lines indicated on pattern, whip a narrow casing to the blouse. Run tape through to tie around waist and control fullness. Close back with buttons and buttonholes. Hem bottom. Make the skirt of a piece of fabric 22¼" x 4". Face the bottom back for 1½" with material to match the blouse. Pleat the skirt in ½" pleats, turned away from a 1½" box pleat in center front. Mount on waistband. Close back with button and buttonhole. Line the suspenders. Sew two sides together except at flat end. Clip corners. Turn and press. Trim all edges with narrow braid. Sew small buttons to dots. Tack pointed end of suspenders to front of skirt as shown. Sew back inside skirt waistband.

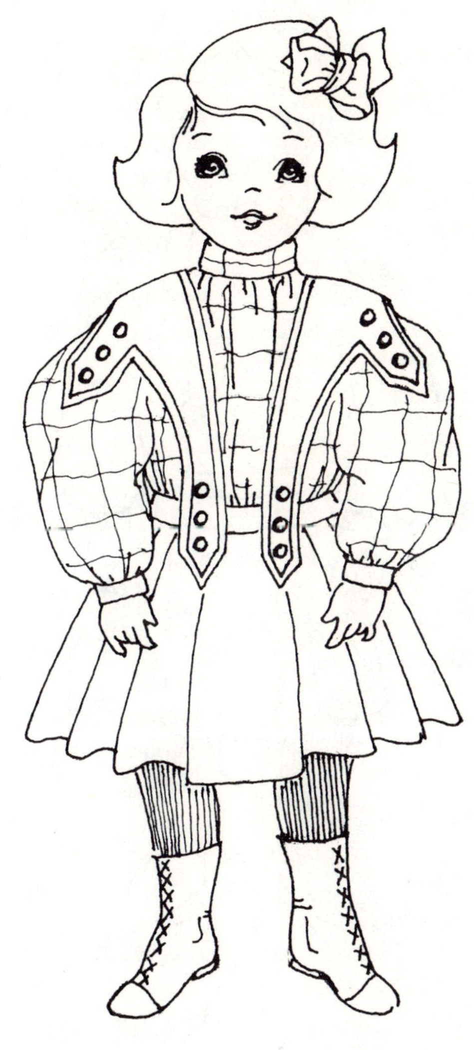

⑫ GREEN PLAID BLOUSE CUFF

CUT TWO

⑫ PLAID BLOUSE - COLLAR - CUT ONE

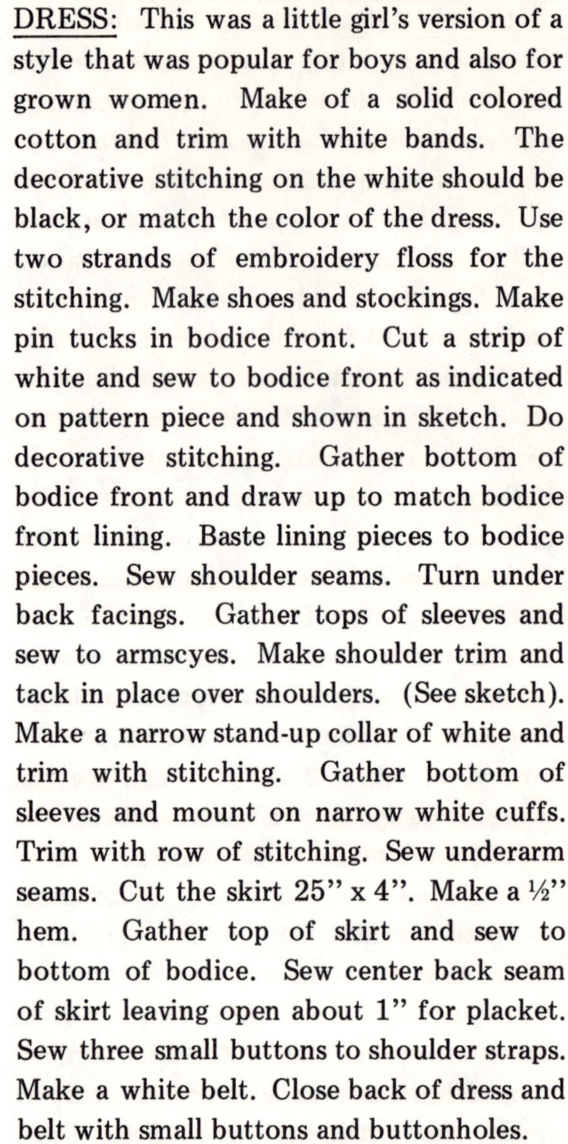

13 - RUSSIAN BLOUSE DRESS: This was a little girl's version of a style that was popular for boys and also for grown women. Make of a solid colored cotton and trim with white bands. The decorative stitching on the white should be black, or match the color of the dress. Use two strands of embroidery floss for the stitching. Make shoes and stockings. Make pin tucks in bodice front. Cut a strip of white and sew to bodice front as indicated on pattern piece and shown in sketch. Do decorative stitching. Gather bottom of bodice front and draw up to match bodice front lining. Baste lining pieces to bodice pieces. Sew shoulder seams. Turn under back facings. Gather tops of sleeves and sew to armscyes. Make shoulder trim and tack in place over shoulders. (See sketch). Make a narrow stand-up collar of white and trim with stitching. Gather bottom of sleeves and mount on narrow white cuffs. Trim with row of stitching. Sew underarm seams. Cut the skirt 25" x 4". Make a ½" hem. Gather top of skirt and sew to bottom of bodice. Sew center back seam of skirt leaving open about 1" for placket. Sew three small buttons to shoulder straps. Make a white belt. Close back of dress and belt with small buttons and buttonholes.

The Wish Booklets are obviously not designed to be cut apart. Trace the patterns onto white tissue paper, making all dots, notches, pleatmarkers, etc. Use an indelible pen or a pencil that will not smudge. Cut the pattern pieces out and pin to muslin. Cut the muslin pieces out and use the muslin as your working pattern. The tissue paper may be filed in an envelope for future reference. Be sure to note any necessary changes before you use the pattern again. Use a dressmaker's pencil to mark directions on the muslin. Small sequin pins are handier for pinning the mock-up together than regular pins.

You can eliminate underarm seams in some bodices and bodice linings by pinning the bodice front and back patterns together along the underarm seam. Be sure all the seam allowance is pinned out. When the patterns are cut this way you have only the shoulder seam to sew. As always, try it in muslin first.

 # 14 - EYELET COAT WITH CAPE: This coat is designed to be made of eyelet edging. The design of the eyelet is the finish for the bottom of the coat, cape, collar and sleeves. Because of this, no seam allowance has been made. If you wish to make the coat of another fabric, please add a sufficient amount of fabric for hems. I made the eyelet coat to be worn with the pink dress with eyelet trim (# 10). I lined the coat with the same pink cotton I had used on the dress. Use 6" wide eyelet for the coat. One yard will be enough. Place bottom of the pattern pieces along the bottom, or scalloped edge - see sketch. Cut a lining for the coat by the same pattern. Press under a narrow hem along the bottom of the skirt. Whip to wrong side of eyelet just above the scallops, where it will not show on the outside. Make inverted box pleats as indicated on the pattern. Baste all remaining lining pieces to corresponding eyelet pieces. Sew front and back yoke pieces to skirt. Turn under facings. Sew shoulder seams. Whip bottom of sleeve linings to bottom of sleeves. Sew sleeve seams. Gather top of sleeves slightly and sew to armscyes. Sew lining to cape. Turn under front facings. Make pleats in cape. Baste cape in place around neck, gathering cape slightly, if necessary, to make it fit properly. Make the collar by mitring a length of eyelet to the shape required. Baste collar in place around neck and then, using a narrow strip of bias batiste, whip raw edges under. Close front with button and loop under collar.

CUTTING DIAGRAM- EYELET COAT

COLLAR
RAW EDGES
BIAS STRIP
INSIDE COAT

15 - DRESS WITH WIDE COLLAR: I made this dress of pale green batiste and trimmed it with eyelet embroidery. It is worn with black stockings and boots. Gather bodice front along double dotted lines and draw up to fit bodice lining. Baste lining pieces to bodice pieces. Sew shoulder seams. Turn under back facings. Sew collars and collar linings together, clip seam, and turn. Trim edges with narrow eyelet edging (lace may also be used) and insertion. Baste collar to bodice, arranging as shown in sketch, with overlap. Sew collar to inside of dress, covering seam with narrow silk ribbon or bias strip. Gather tops of sleeves and sew to armscyes. Gather bottoms of sleeves and finish with eyelet ruffle and insertion. Sew underarm seam. Sew a row of insertion around waist. Place the top edge of the insertion over gathering thread. Cut the skirt 25" x 4". Gather the top to fit the waist and sew together. Trim excess seam allowance away under insertions. Sew center back seam and make a ½" hem in bottom. Close back with four buttons and buttonholes.

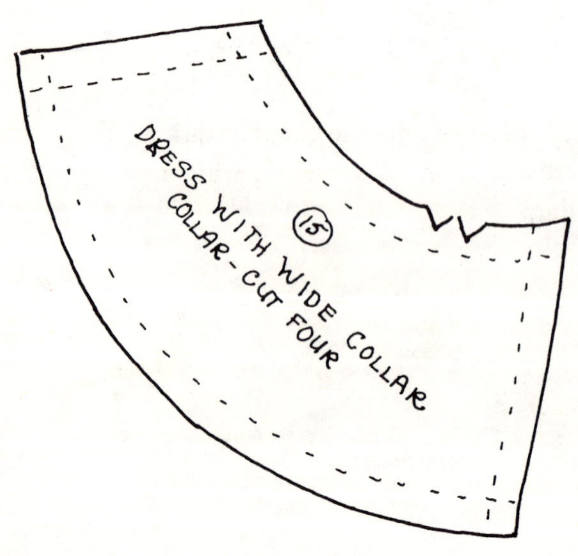

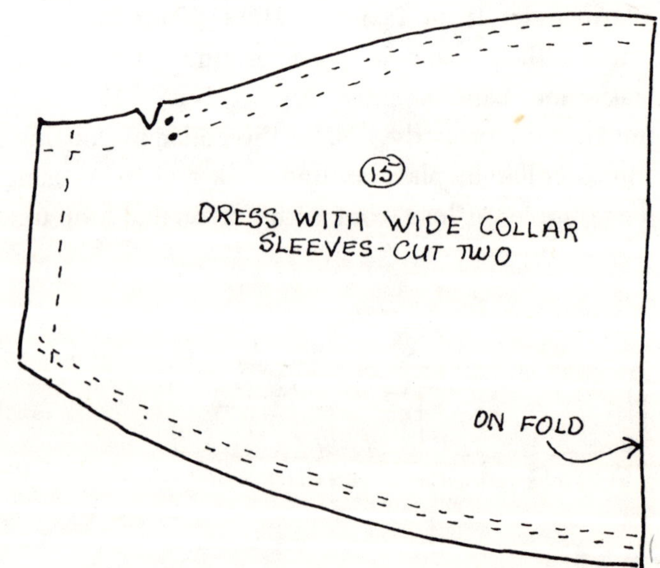

16 - EMPIRE DRESS: This dress does not require a lining. Make the yoke of lace or eyelet and the dress of china silk, lightweight wool or cotton. The neck and sleeves are finished with a narrow lace frill. Gather tops of bodice pieces and sew to bottom of yoke pieces. Sew shoulder seams. Gather tops of sleeves and sew to armscyes. Gather bottom of sleeves and narrowly bind. Trim binding with narrow frill of lace. Sew underarm seams. Gather bottom of bodice and sew a strip of of ½" insertion over gathering thread. Cut the skirt 25" x 5". Gather top of skirt to fit bottom of bodice. Sew bottom of row of insertion over gathering stitches. Trim excess seam allowance away under insertion. Sew center back seam, leaving about 1½" open below the belt. Turn under back facing. Narrowly bind neck and edge with frill of narrow lace. Make a ½" hem in bottom of dress. Close back with three buttons and buttonholes. NOTE: The yoke and belt may be made of self-material and worked with a simple braiding pattern.

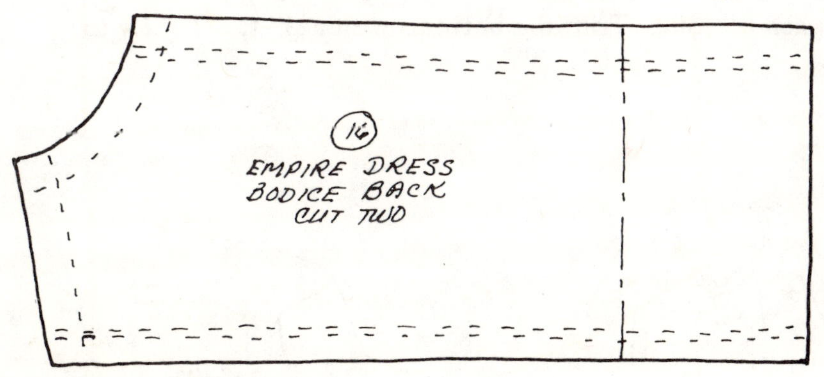

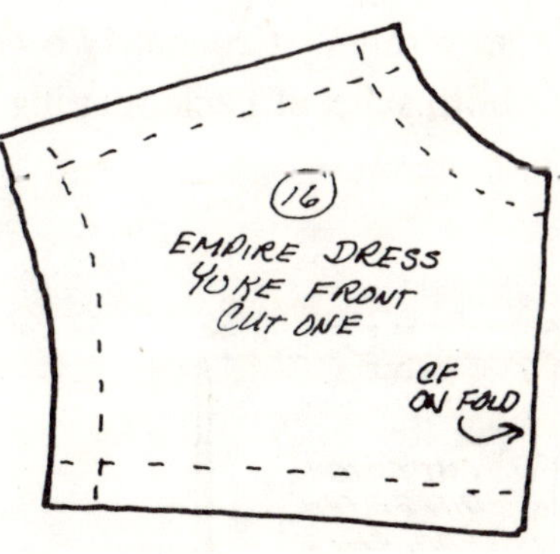

17 - CIRCULAR CAPE WITH COLLAR OR HOOD: Make the cape of cream-colored broadcloth or very light-weight wool. Line it with pale pink cotton satin. The ties may be made of cream-colored crochet thread. If you use the collar, omit the hood. Fold the material for the cape into quarters so that you can cut a circle. See cutting diagram. Cut a circle for the neck and cut the front open all the way. Make sure that the straight of the material is in the front. Cut the lining to match the cape. Sew them together, right sides facing on all except neck edges. Trim seams, clip curves, turn and press. Sew the outside edges of the collar pieces together. Leave neck edge open. Clip corners, turn and press. Place the underside of the collar around the neck edge and sew in place. Turn under seam allowance on upper side of collar and sew to inside of cape, concealing raw seams. To make a hood instead of the collar, cut one hood of cream and one of pink. With right sides facing, sew the two pieces together along the straight (or face) edge. Gather the curved edge and draw up to fit neck of cape. Sew the two together and conceal raw edges on inside of cape with silk ribbon or narrow bias strip. Gather face edge and draw up so that it fits around the doll's head, but not too snugly. Sew a piece of silk ribbon over gathers inside to stay them. Crochet two chains, each 5" long. Trim the bottoms with a ½" tassel. Sew to both sides of neck opening for ties.

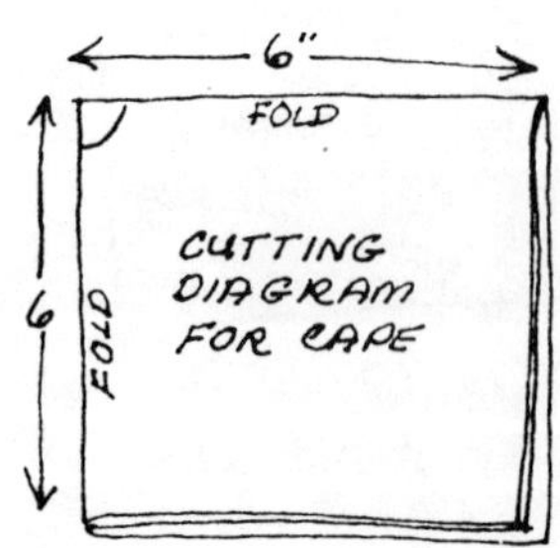

BACK VIEW OF CAPE WITH HOOD

SEWING THE COLLAR TO CAPE

18 - DRESS WITH BERTHA:

This dress may be made of nainsook or batiste, trimmed with Val lace insertion and edging, and tucks. Before you begin to cut the pattern pieces, make pintucks and set in insertion on a 5" x 6" piece of fabric. Cut the yoke front and back, matching the tucks and insertion on shoulder seams. Sew shoulder seams. Narrowly bind bottom of yoke. Make tuck in bertha pieces. Sew center front seam on bertha. Edge bertha with lace. Trim bertha as shown with two rows of feather-stitching. When the bertha construction is completed, gather the top of it to fit the bottom of the yoke. Sew bodice shoulder seams. Gather tops of sleeves to fit armscyes and sew sleeves in place. Gather bottoms of sleeves to fit doll and make cuffs of lace insertion. Sew underarm seams. Make tucks in bodice backs and gather bodice front to fit bottom of yoke. Baste top of bertha to top of bodice. Place bottom of yoke over gathering thread in bertha and bodice; slip-stitch in place. Hem back facings in place. Sew a strip of insertion edged on top with lace around neck for collar. Mount bodice on lining. Cut lining away under yoke and slip-stitch edge of lining to yoke seam. Make the skirt 24" x 5". Sew center back seam, leaving about 1" open for placket. Hem placket. Make a ½" hem in bottom and trim as shown with a row of feather-stitching. Gather to fit bottom of bodice. Slip-stitch bodice to skirt. Close back with buttons and buttonholes.

Times change and costs keep pace. In 1908 lawn was 16¢ a yard, cotton insertion was 8¢ a yard, cambric was 14¢ a yard, buttons were a penny a piece and thread was 6¢ a spool. The price of sewing, like the price of dolls, has gone up!

In order to cut down on your expenditures for individual doll dresses, measure your muslin mock-up so you know how much fabric and trim to buy. Of course, if you are like all the rest of us, you can't do that because you have stacks of material you have bought and saved because "it might come in handy some day".

19 - HANGING DRESS: This dress may be made of white batiste and trimmed with Val lace and insertion. The yoke and cuffs, instead of being formed with insertion, may be made of self-material edged with a narrow lace ruffle. The dress should be worn with black shoes and socks. Make the yoke of ½" insertion. First cut a brown paper yoke following the yoke pattern. Pin the shoulder seams together and cut the yoke in one piece, omitting the back facing. Baste the three rows of lace for the yoke to the brown paper. Drawing up the upper marginal thread in the insertion, make the three rows fit one another. Remove basting thread to release yoke from brown paper. Make pleats in dress front and back. Sew shoulder seams. Sew bottom of yoke to top of dress. Gather top of sleeves to fit armscyes. Sew in place. Gather bottom of sleeves to fit doll. Mount on cuff made of lace insertion. Sew underarm seam. Face back edges of insertion with a piece of lace, or net, or self-fabric. Turn under back facing of dress. Sew center back seam. Hem dress. Sew a narrow lace ruffle around neck and bottom of sleeves. Make a ruffle from a strip of self-material 1" wide and 25" long. Edge the bottom with lace. Gather the top to fit around dress just above hemline and baste in place. Conceal raw edges by whipping a row of lace insertion over it. Close back with three buttons and buttonholes. This dress may also have a sash tied around the waist.

These rather simple dresses were only one or two years removed in style from the infant's long dress. They were more suited to the two or three year olds, although they were also worn by older children. The hanging dress was always made in white during this period.

In case you have been wondering how all the white garments stayed white, they could be rubbed with magnesia after each wearing. The chemical was brushed off prior to the next wearing. All the dirt and grey went with the magnesia. This treatment was for silk, wool and crepe. Cotton, naturally, was washed on Mondays and ironed on Tuesdays.

20 - BLACK VELVET COAT TRIMMED WITH ERMINE: This very fetching coat can be made of velveteen, wool or linen. It should be trimmed with velvet to simulate fur. The velvet which is most generally available is made of rayon. The facing and bindings must be made of lightweight silk. Every step possible should be taken to reduce bulk. Velveteen should be cut just below the hemline. There will be much less bulk if the hem is faced with silk. Seams can be buttonhole-stitched together to reduce bulk and raveling. The collar and cuffs should be faced with white silk. The velveteen cape collar need not be lined at all. If you make the coat of linen, it may be trimmed with lace. A woolen coat could be trimmed with braid. Make pleats in fronts and backs. Sew to bottom of yoke. Sew shoulder seams. Sew front facings to coat. If the coat is of linen or wool, line the cape collar. Otherwise, bind as narrowly as possible with white velvet. Baste in place around neck and narrowly bind. Sew underarm seam. Work "ermine" on velvet using lazy-daisy-stitch. Line velvet with white silk and tack in place around neck and at sleeve bottoms. Turn up hem. Close with a hook and eye under collar and snaps down front. Sew small pearl buttons where shown. If you're very good, you can work buttonholes!

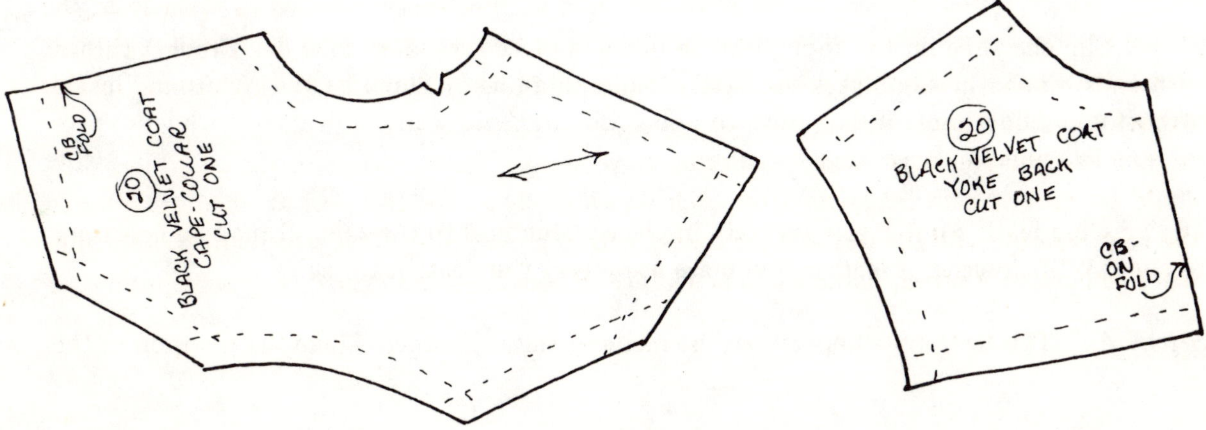

SHOES, BOOTS AND LEGGINGS

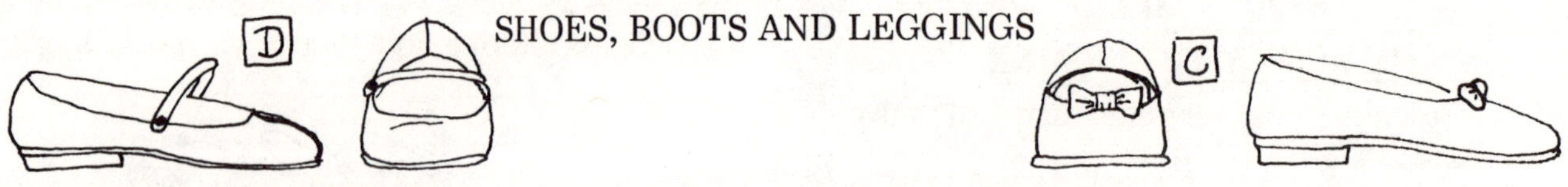

General Directions for Making Shoes

1 - The shoes may be made in black or white leather, or pastel fabric — silk or cotton — to match the dresses or the sash on white dresses.

2 - Trace pattern pieces onto an index card or other fairly heavy paper. First make the shoes in brown paper, gluing seams together. This will assure you that the shoe will fit.

3 - Cut two insoles of cardboard and two outer soles of fairly heavy black or brown leather. Make sure that the edges are cleanly cut.

4 - Cut two heels of leather to match the outer soles.

5 - Press the fabric for the uppers onto the lightest weight STAFLEX. If you are using kid you may also use the STAFLEX to make the leather more solid.

6 - Blanket-stitch all UNSEAMED edges. Use silk twist, buttonhole twist or embroidery floss - two strands. If you wish, the edges may be finished with a very narrow binding of silk ribbon instead of blanket-stitching. Binding can frequently be glued on.

7 - Work eyelets wherever they are needed. Punch a *small* hole with an awl. Work the buttonhole stitches around the hole. KEEP THE HOLE SMALL. It should not be much larger than the lace or button it must accommodate.

8 - Sew seams. Notice that the seam allowance is narrow. Place right sides together and blanket-stitch. You may, if you prefer, shave the thickness of leather uppers at the edge and glue the edges together by overlapping the shaved edges. If you do this, you may have to touch up the seam a little with some paint just at the edge. This is particularly true if you are working with black.

9 - Slip the shoe on the foot. Button or tie in place according to style. Crochet thread with ends dipped in wax makes good ties. Run a thin line of Elmer's Glue-All around inside of bottom. Slide insole inside, next to doll's foot and fold seam allowance (with glue) over the sole and glue in place.

10 - Glue leather outer sole securely in place. Glue heel to the sole. It may be necessary to cut two thicknesses of leather if you are using very thin leather for soles.

SHOE A - The bedroom slippers may be made of silk or flannel. Make the pompon of the finest baby yarn and glue in place. The pompon can be made by wrapping yarn around a Dritz sewing guage. Tie in the center. Clip ends to remove and then trim into a ball if necessary. Omit heels.

SHOE B - This is one of the typical shoes found on dolls of this period. The originals are frequently of a black fabric somewhat resembling oil cloth. Follow general directions. Purchase two small buckles for the instep. Thread the instep trim through the buckle and glue to instep.

SHOE C - Trim this shoe just on the instep with a tiny bow of self-material if the shoes are made of silk or fabric, or silk ribbon if they are made of leather. To make the bow, cut a narrow strip of fabric on the bias. Turn under and glue narrow hems along each edge. Fold ends under and fasten in center with a tiny snip of fabric.

SHOE D - Use the pattern for shoe C to make shoe D except add a narrow strap across the instep. This pattern may be further varied by making a small bow for the instep, or larger one of silk ribbon for the strap.

SHOE E - Sew toe to shoe before blanket-stitching but after working buttonholes. Do not buttonhole tongue. Glue it underneath opening to toe after boot is completed. Match X's. This boot seems always to have been made of black leather.

SHOE F - Sew center front seam. Work buttonholes and sew buttons on. Button. Sew bottom part to upper. This boot was seen in shiny black leather with cloth uppers.

SHOE G - The leggings are made either in black or white kid or cloth. They may be worn over the little pump (shoe C). Sew center front seam. Make buttonholes and sew on buttons. Sew narrow elastic under instep.

HAIR, BOWS AND BONNETS

By far, the most common adornment for the head was a large bow perched on one side or the other, or squarely at the top. Suggestions for ways of arranging your doll's hair are drawn on the dolls in the booklet. The most popular styles were the short bob, with the top drawn back and secured by a bow, and the long ringlets.

Hats in this period were big floppy things with big bows and big clusters of flowers. Basically the shape was the same; the big brim and the upright crown were component parts. Sometimes the underside of the brim was lined with matching and other times contrasting fabric. Velvet or silk ribbon was used to outline the brim. The eyelet mob cap seems to have been very popular. It was usually trimmed with ribbons, although occasionally a cluster of flowers replaced the bow.

HAT # 1 - This all-purpose summer bonnet may be made to wear with any of the lace trimmed frocks. It is illustrated on dress # 10, the pink dress. Make the bonnet of 3" eyelet edging. Cut it 20" long. Seam the two ends together. Gather the top edge into a tight circle. Run a gathering thread around the bonnet 1½" above the lower edge and draw up to fit doll's head. Tie a bow of ribbon around the gathering thread and tack in place.

HAT # 2 - This hat is shown with the eyelet coat, # 14. It is made of straw and trimmed with flowers and ribbon bows. Construct the hat form of index card. Use magic mending tape to hold the pieces together. Soak narrow straw in warm water. Baste a row of straw to the outside of the brim. Do not cut straw. Continue sewing the straw round and round, whipping each row to the one preceding it. Do not sew the straw to the cardboard form. When the form is completely covered, tuck the end to the inside and secure. Bend the brim up in the front and tape in place. Let the hat dry completely. Remove from form and spray with clear plastic spray. Trim hat on brim with a large cluster of flowers on the side and front of crown. Tie three bows of ½" ribbon and trim back of crown with them.

HAT # 3 - Hat # 3 is made with the same pattern as hat # 2 and is shown with the cape, # 17. Construct the hat form of index card, again using magic mending tape to join the pieces. Cover the form with silk or velvet or both. Cut a piece to cover the crown and sew that in place. Then, cut the circular brim. Use the form pattern but add an outside seam allowance. Baste the seam allowance around the outside of the brim. Then trim under the inside seam allowance and whip edge to bottom of crown covering. Cut a small circle to cover the top of the crown. Turn under seam allowance and whip in place around edge. Cut another brim covering for the underside of brim. Baste under seam allowance. Pin to brim and slip-stitch to the upper brim covering. Remove the basting threads. Cut a circle large enough to fit inside the crown, gathering it around edge of brim to fit snugly. Turn under seam allowance and whip crown lining to the underside of brim. *NOTE:* The object of covering the form is to do it as snugly and wrinkle-free as possible. At first, this is accomplished through trial and error. Practice before you cut into a good piece of fabric. Try to keep your stitches invisible. Trim hat # 3 with large loops of 1" ribbon arranged around the brim and a bow of ½" lace tucked under the front of the brim, which should be turned up a little in the front.

<u>*HAT # 4*</u> - Use hat # 3 crown pattern for this hat which is pictured with the black velvet coat, # 20. For the winter, the hat can be made of velvet and for the summer, of straw. Make it according to previous directions and tie a 1" wide ribbon around crown, making a large bow in front.

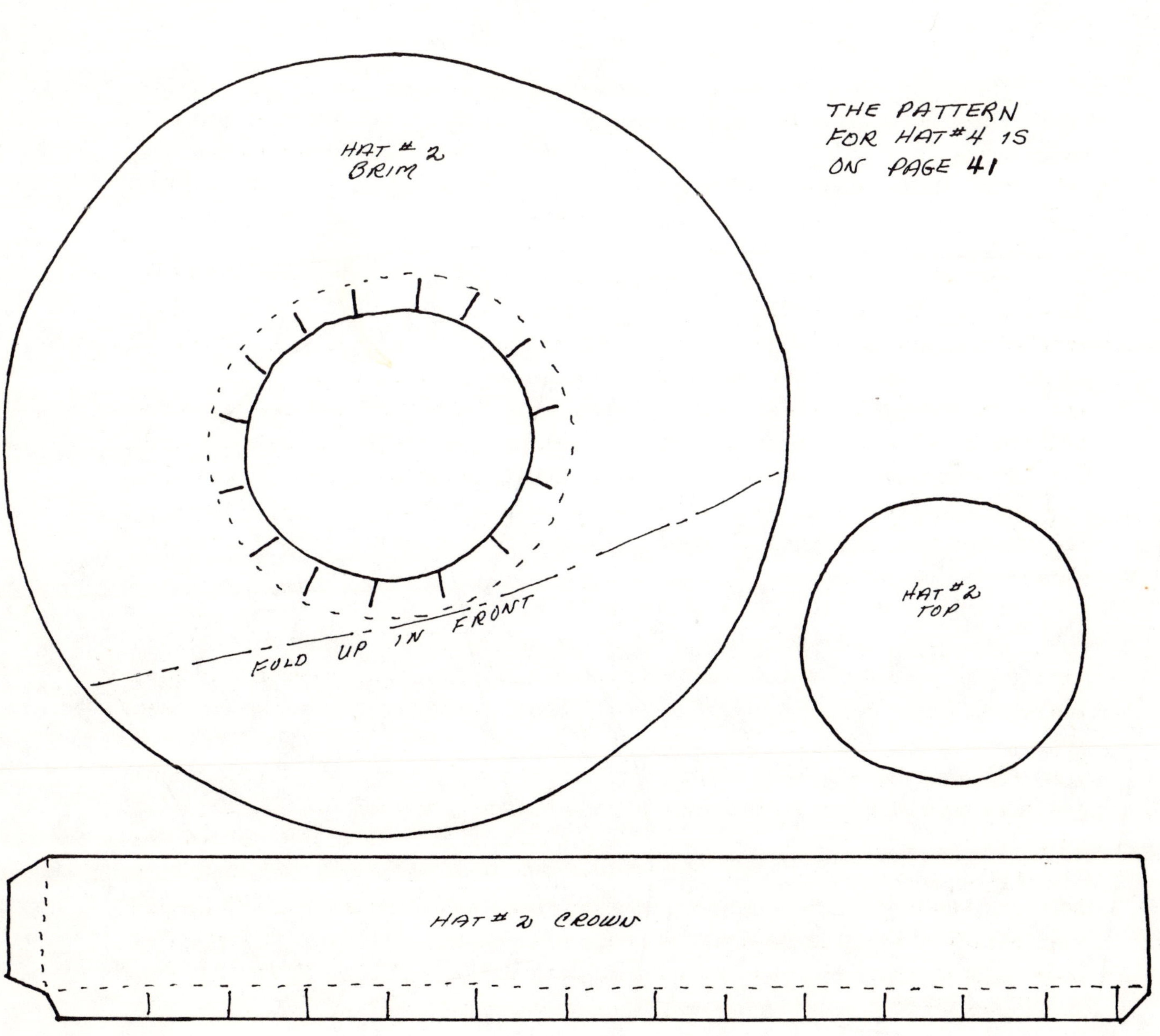

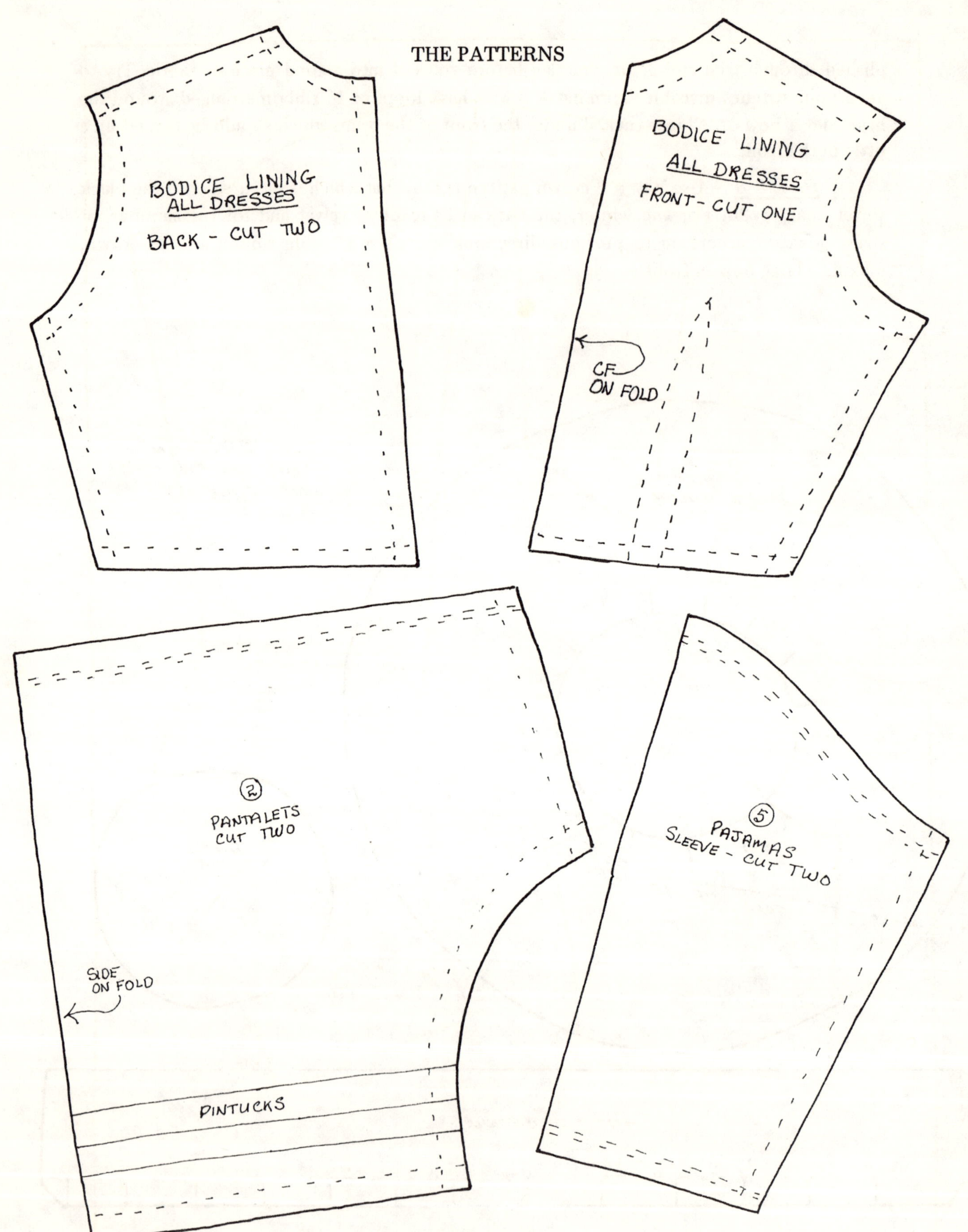
BODICE LINING
ALL DRESSES
BACK - CUT TWO
BODICE LINING
ALL DRESSES
FRONT - CUT ONE
CF
ON FOLD
②
PANTALETS
CUT TWO
SIDE
ON FOLD
PINTUCKS
⑤
PAJAMAS
SLEEVE - CUT TWO

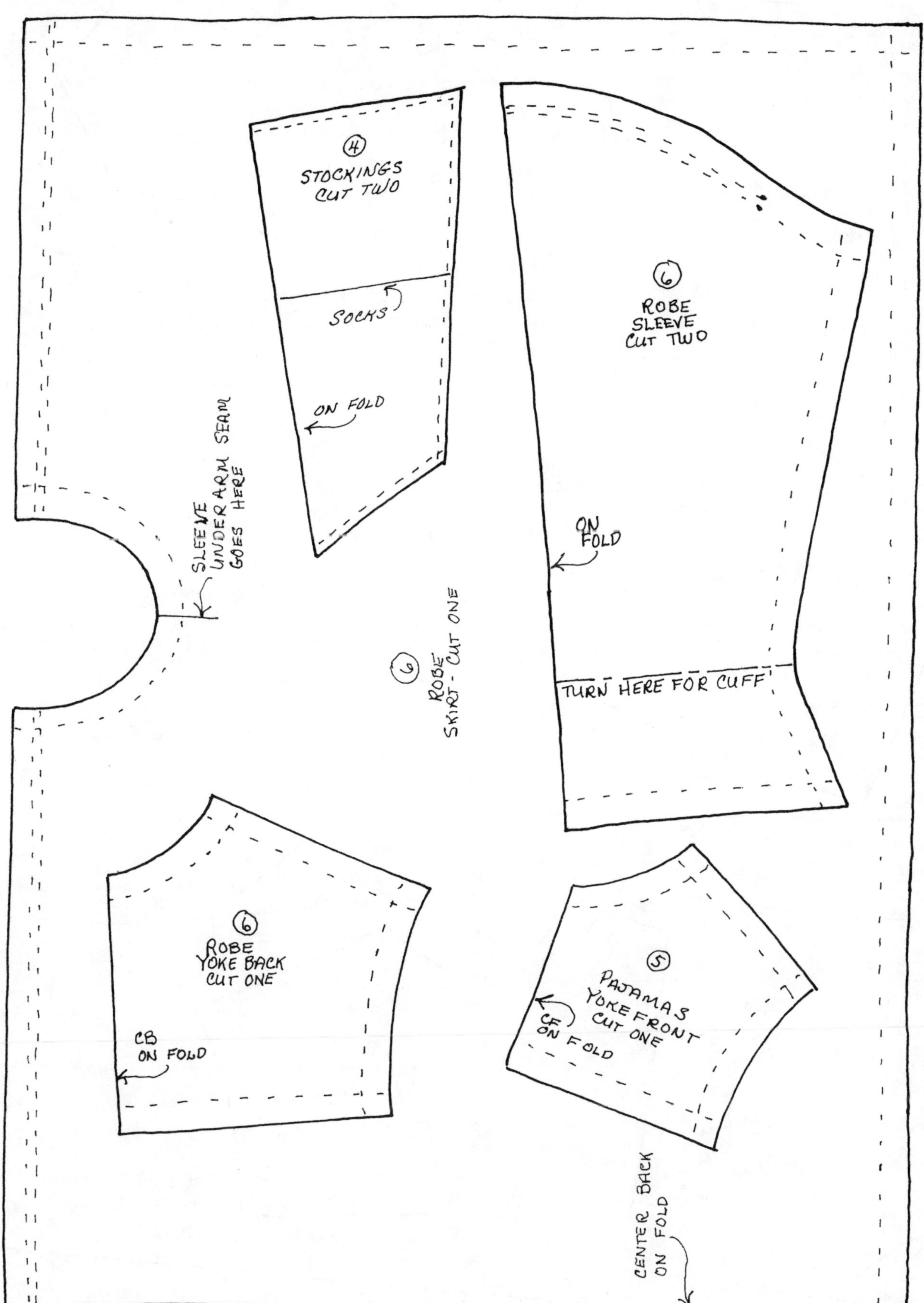
④
STOCKINGS
CUT TWO
SOCKS
ON FOLD
⑥
ROBE
SLEEVE
CUT TWO
ON FOLD
TURN HERE FOR CUFF
SLEEVE
UNDERARM SEAM
GOES HERE
⑥
ROBE
SKIRT - CUT ONE
⑥
ROBE
YOKE BACK
CUT ONE
CB
ON FOLD
⑤
PAJAMAS
YOKE FRONT
CUT ONE
CF
ON FOLD
CENTER BACK
ON FOLD

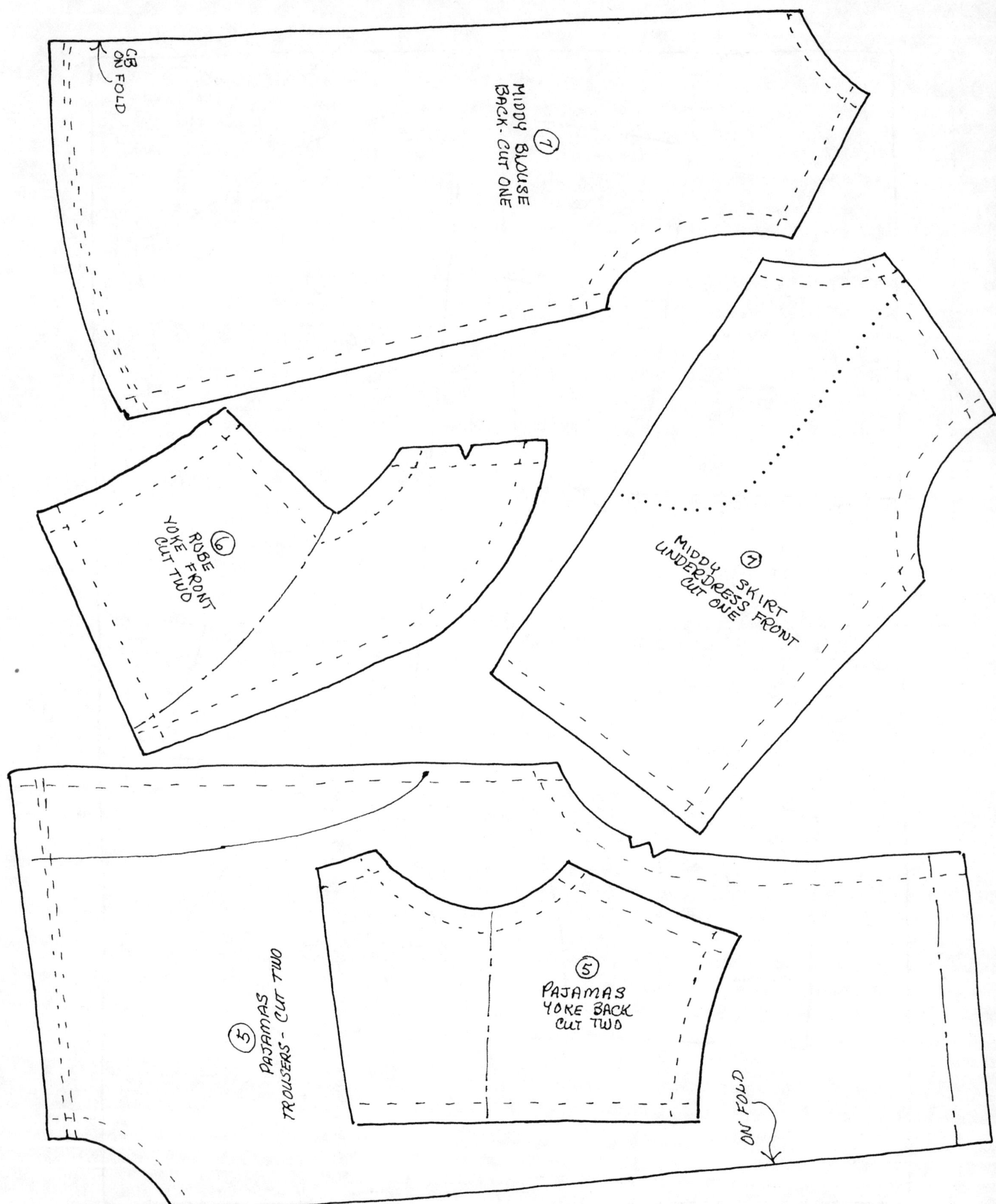
CB ON FOLD
7 MIDDY BLOUSE BACK - CUT ONE
6 ROBE YOKE FRONT CUT TWO
7 MIDDY SKIRT UNDERDRESS FRONT CUT ONE
5 PAJAMAS TROUSERS - CUT TWO
5 PAJAMAS YOKE BACK CUT TWO
ON FOLD

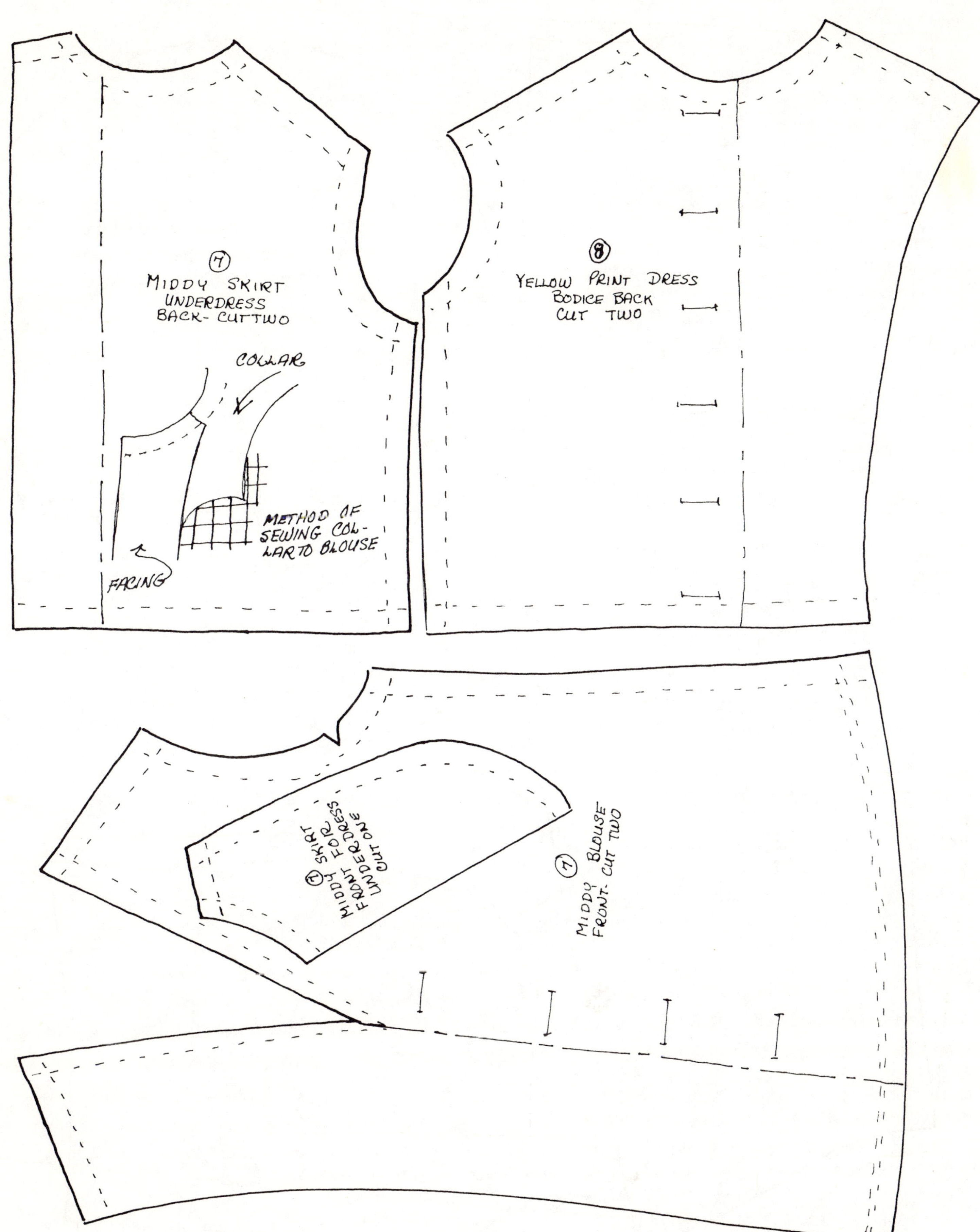
7
MIDDY SKIRT
UNDERDRESS
BACK- CUT TWO
COLLAR
METHOD OF
SEWING COL-
LAR TO BLOUSE
FACING
8
YELLOW PRINT DRESS
BODICE BACK
CUT TWO
7 SKIRT
MIDDY FOR DRESS
FRONT UNDER ONE
CUT ONE
7 BLOUSE
MIDDY CUT TWO
FRONT-

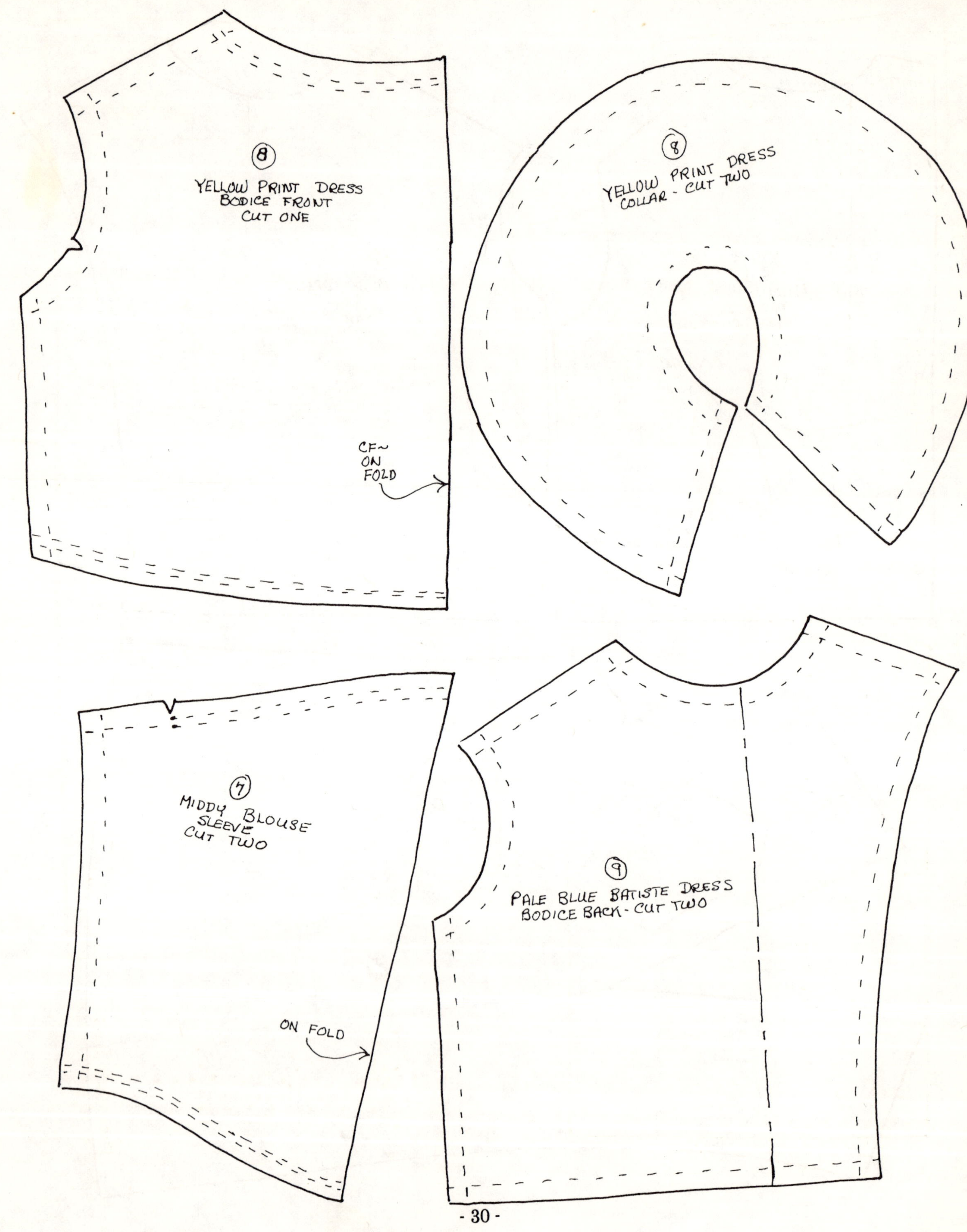
8
YELLOW PRINT DRESS
BODICE FRONT
CUT ONE
CF~
ON
FOLD
8
YELLOW PRINT DRESS
COLLAR - CUT TWO
7
MIDDY BLOUSE
SLEEVE
CUT TWO
ON FOLD
9
PALE BLUE BATISTE DRESS
BODICE BACK - CUT TWO

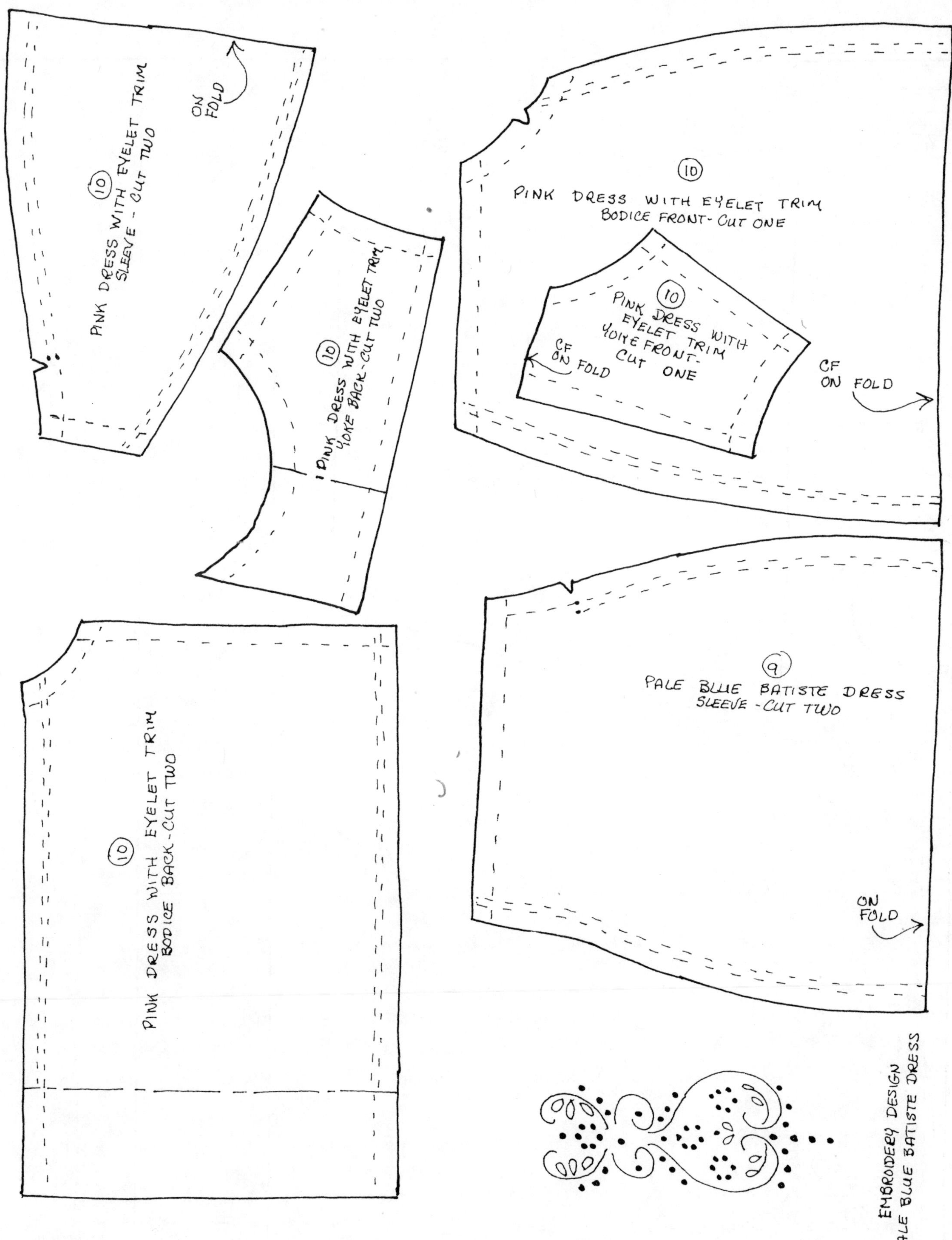
ON FOLD
(10) PINK DRESS WITH EYELET TRIM
SLEEVE - CUT TWO
(10) PINK DRESS WITH EYELET TRIM
YOKE BACK - CUT TWO
(10)
PINK DRESS WITH EYELET TRIM
BODICE FRONT - CUT ONE
(10) PINK DRESS WITH EYELET TRIM
YOKE FRONT - CUT ONE
CF ON FOLD
CF ON FOLD
(10) PINK DRESS WITH EYELET TRIM
BODICE BACK - CUT TWO
(9)
PALE BLUE BATISTE DRESS
SLEEVE - CUT TWO
ON FOLD
EMBROIDERY DESIGN
PALE BLUE BATISTE DRESS

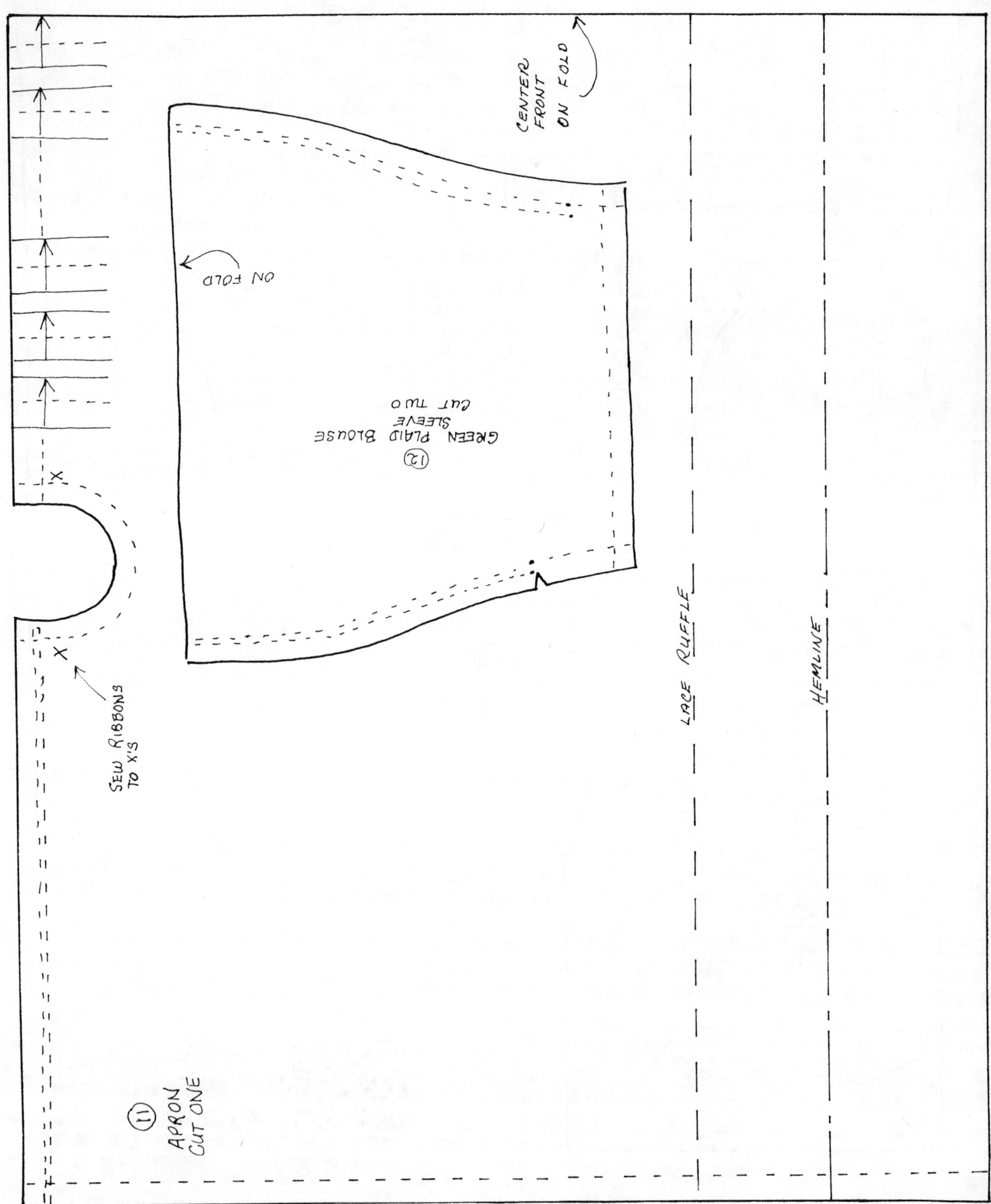
CENTER FRONT ON FOLD
ON FOLD
⑫ GREEN PLAID BLOUSE
SLEEVE
CUT TWO
LACE RUFFLE
HEMLINE
SEW RIBBONS TO X'S
⑪ APRON
CUT ONE

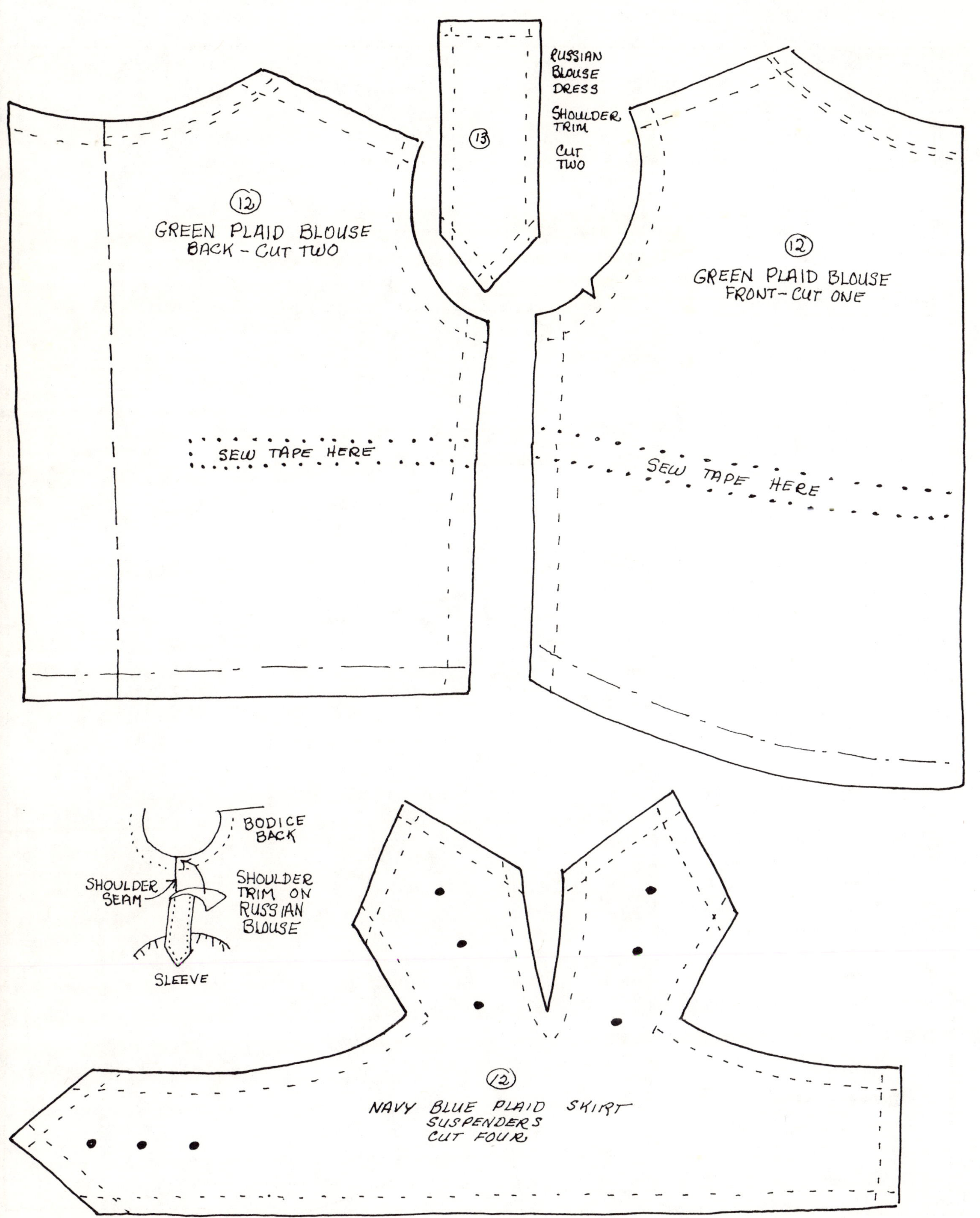
RUSSIAN
BLOUSE
DRESS
SHOULDER
TRIM
CUT
TWO
13
12
GREEN PLAID BLOUSE
BACK - CUT TWO
12
GREEN PLAID BLOUSE
FRONT - CUT ONE
SEW TAPE HERE
SEW TAPE HERE
BODICE
BACK
SHOULDER
SEAM
SHOULDER
TRIM ON
RUSSIAN
BLOUSE
SLEEVE
12
NAVY BLUE PLAID SKIRT
SUSPENDERS
CUT FOUR

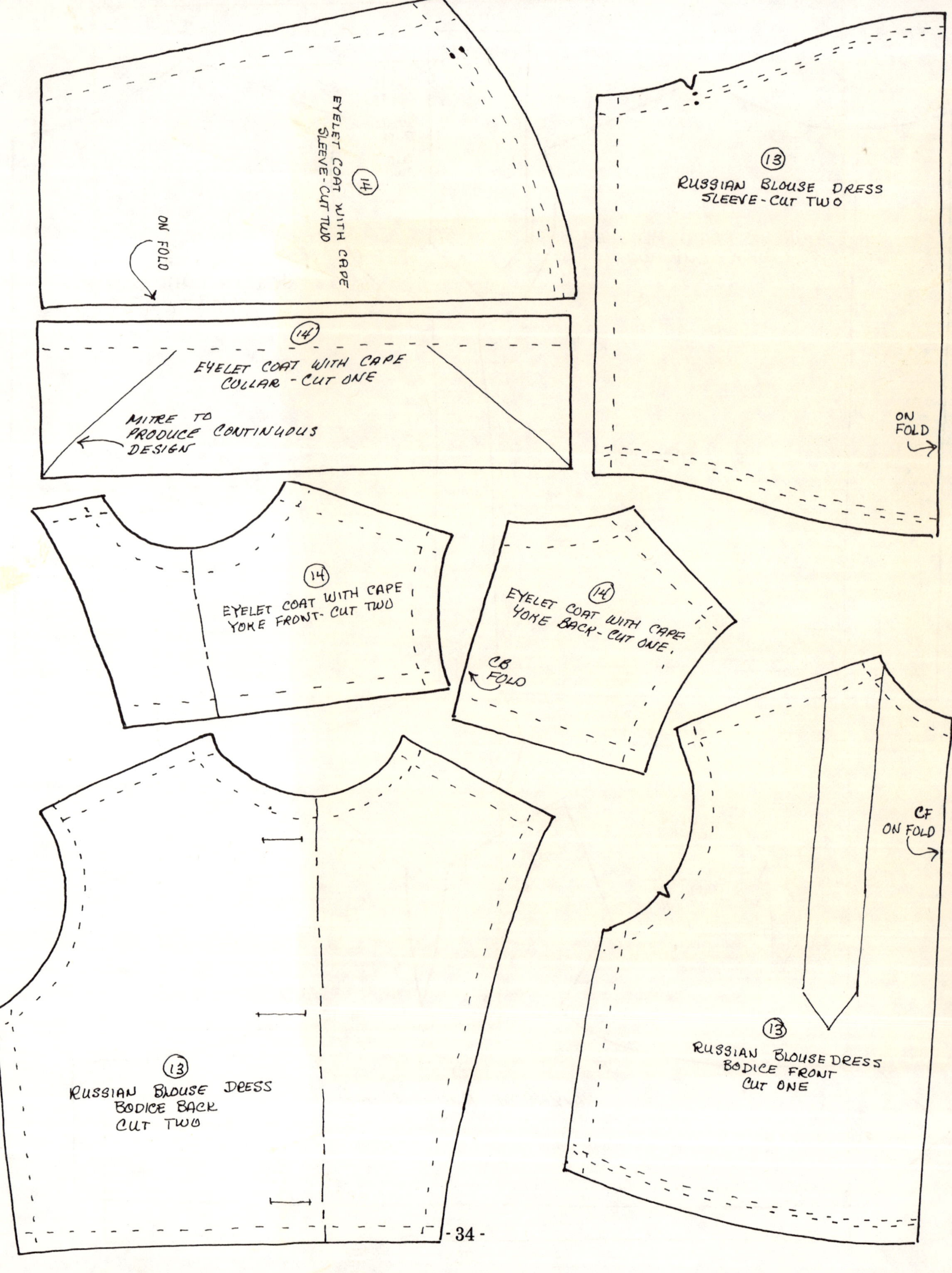

14
EYELET COAT WITH CAPE
SLEEVE-CUT TWO
ON FOLD
13
RUSSIAN BLOUSE DRESS
SLEEVE-CUT TWO
ON FOLD
14
EYELET COAT WITH CAPE
COLLAR - CUT ONE
MITRE TO
PRODUCE CONTINUOUS
DESIGN
14
EYELET COAT WITH CAPE
YOKE FRONT- CUT TWO
14
EYELET COAT WITH CAPE
YOKE BACK- CUT ONE.
CB
FOLD
CF
ON FOLD
13
RUSSIAN BLOUSE DRESS
BODICE BACK
CUT TWO
13
RUSSIAN BLOUSE DRESS
BODICE FRONT
CUT ONE

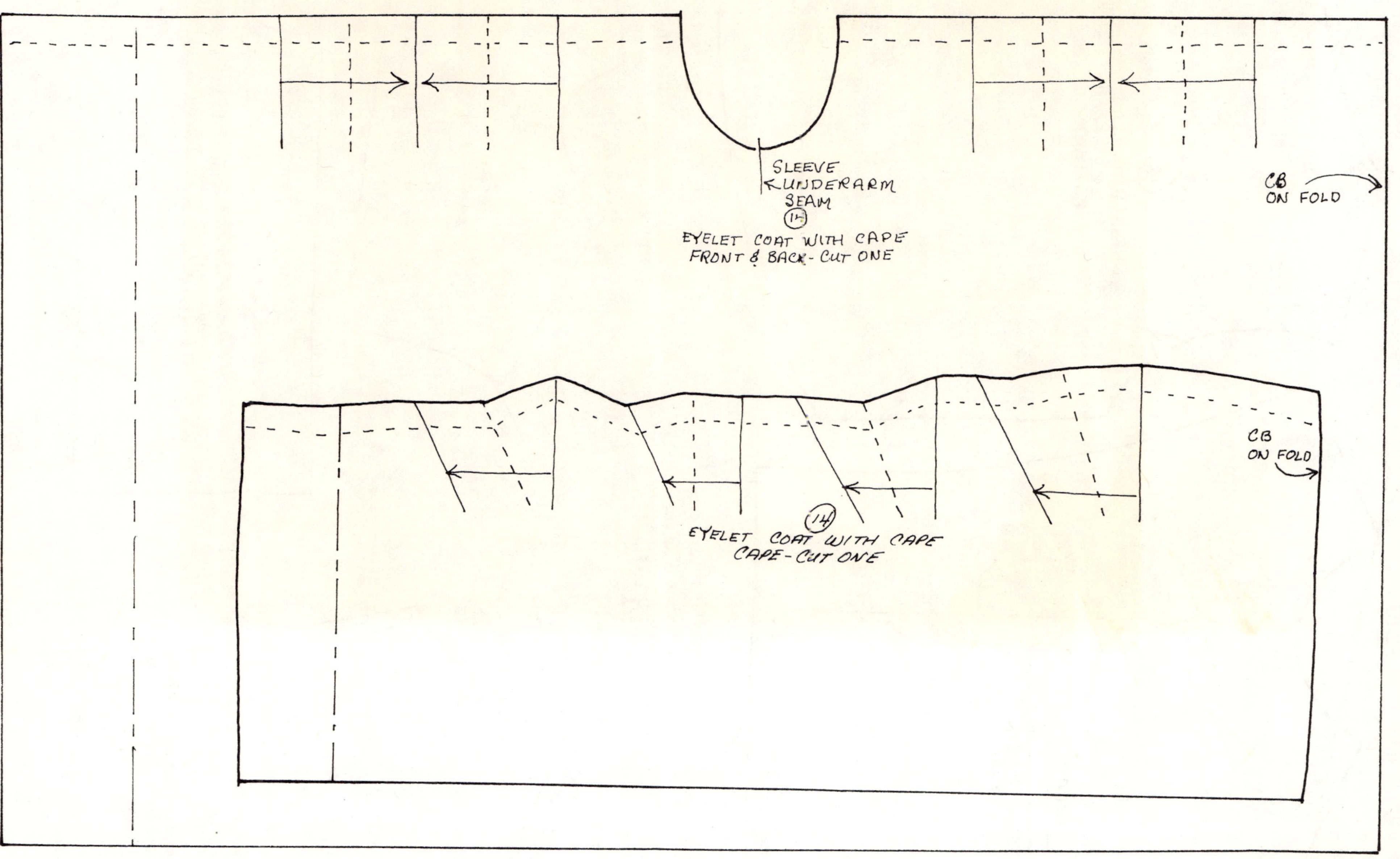
SLEEVE
UNDERARM
SEAM
EYELET COAT WITH CAPE
FRONT & BACK - CUT ONE
CB
ON FOLD
CB
ON FOLD
14
EYELET COAT WITH CAPE
CAPE - CUT ONE

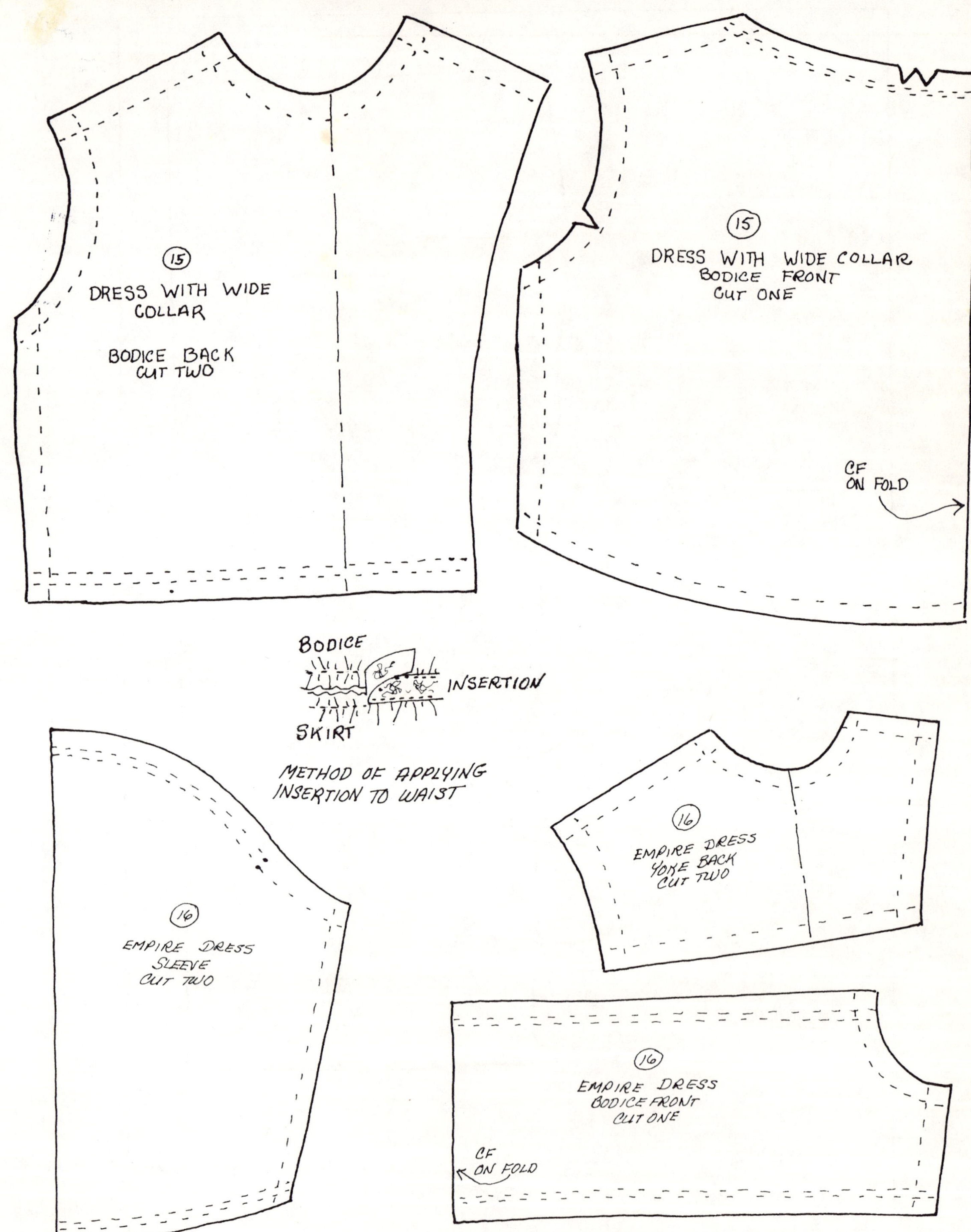
15
DRESS WITH WIDE COLLAR
BODICE BACK
CUT TWO
15
DRESS WITH WIDE COLLAR
BODICE FRONT
CUT ONE
CF
ON FOLD
BODICE
INSERTION
SKIRT
METHOD OF APPLYING
INSERTION TO WAIST
16
EMPIRE DRESS
SLEEVE
CUT TWO
16
EMPIRE DRESS
YOKE BACK
CUT TWO
16
EMPIRE DRESS
BODICE FRONT
CUT ONE
CF
ON FOLD

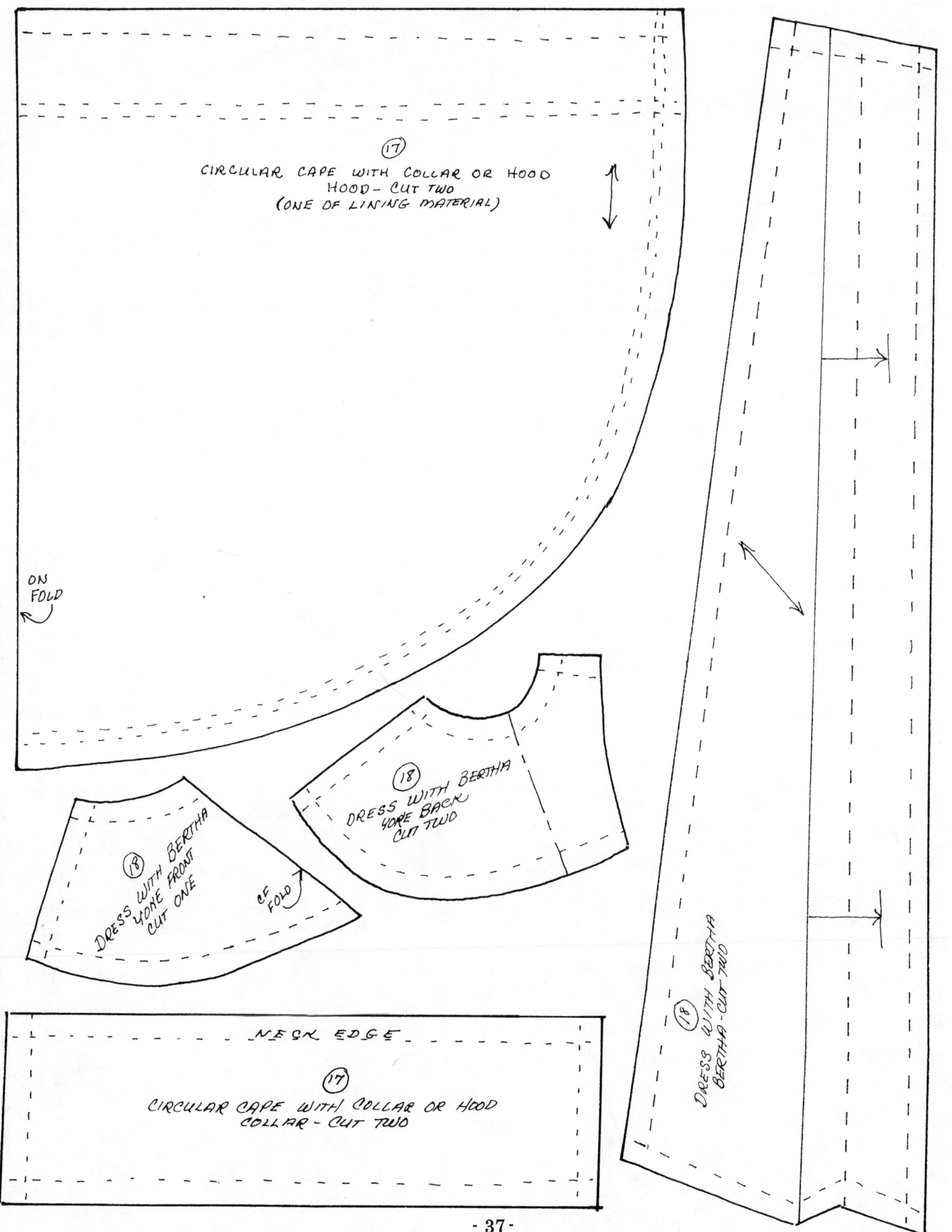
17
CIRCULAR CAPE WITH COLLAR OR HOOD
HOOD- CUT TWO
(ONE OF LINING MATERIAL)
ON FOLD
18
DRESS WITH BERTHA
YOKE BACK
CUT TWO
18
DRESS WITH BERTHA
YOKE FRONT
CUT ONE
CF FOLD
18
DRESS WITH BERTHA
BERTHA-CUT TWO
NECK EDGE
17
CIRCULAR CAPE WITH COLLAR OR HOOD
COLLAR - CUT TWO

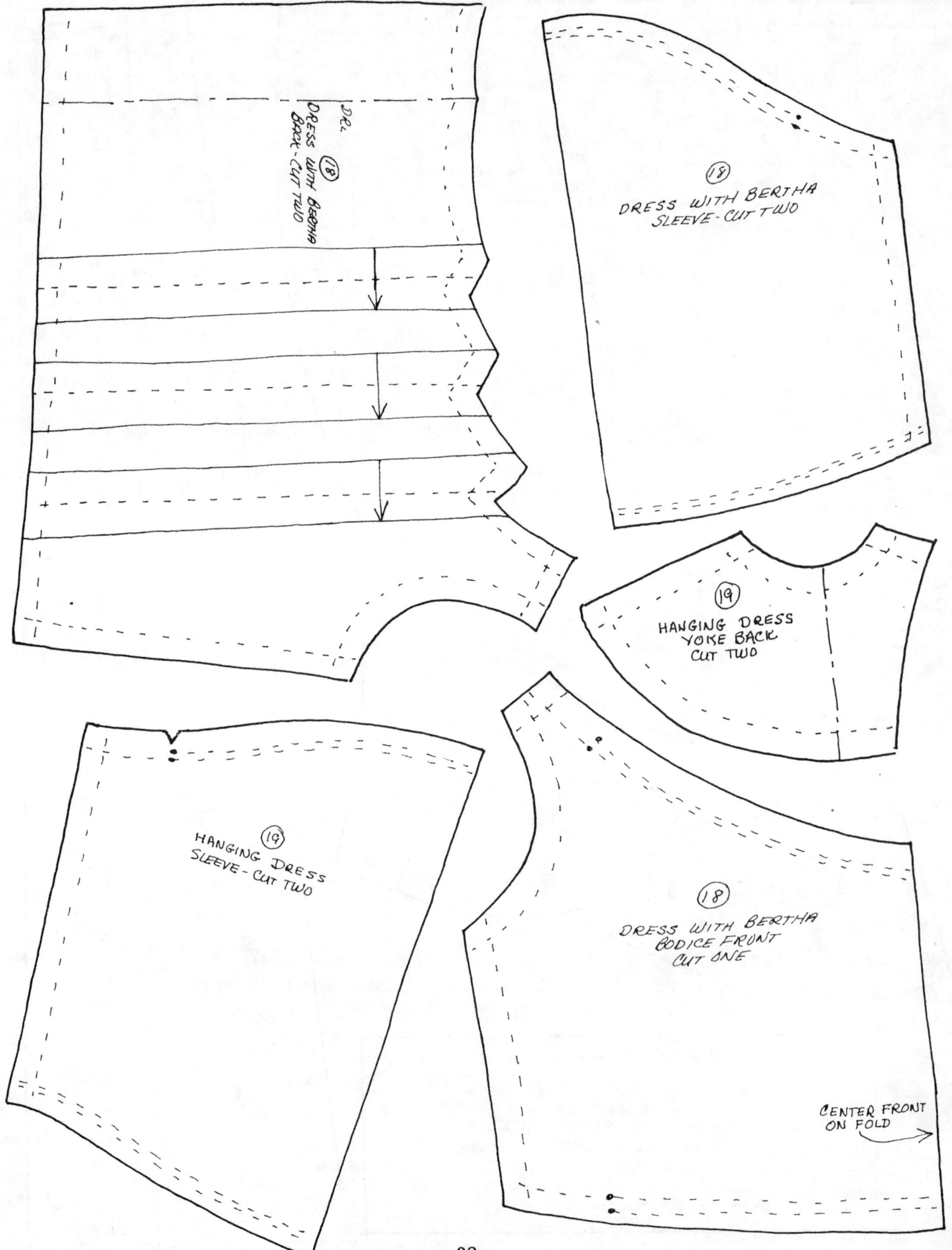
DRESS WITH BERTHA
BACK-CUT TWO
18
DRESS WITH BERTHA
SLEEVE-CUT TWO
19
HANGING DRESS
YOKE BACK
CUT TWO
19
HANGING DRESS
SLEEVE-CUT TWO
18
DRESS WITH BERTHA
BODICE FRONT
CUT ONE
CENTER FRONT
ON FOLD

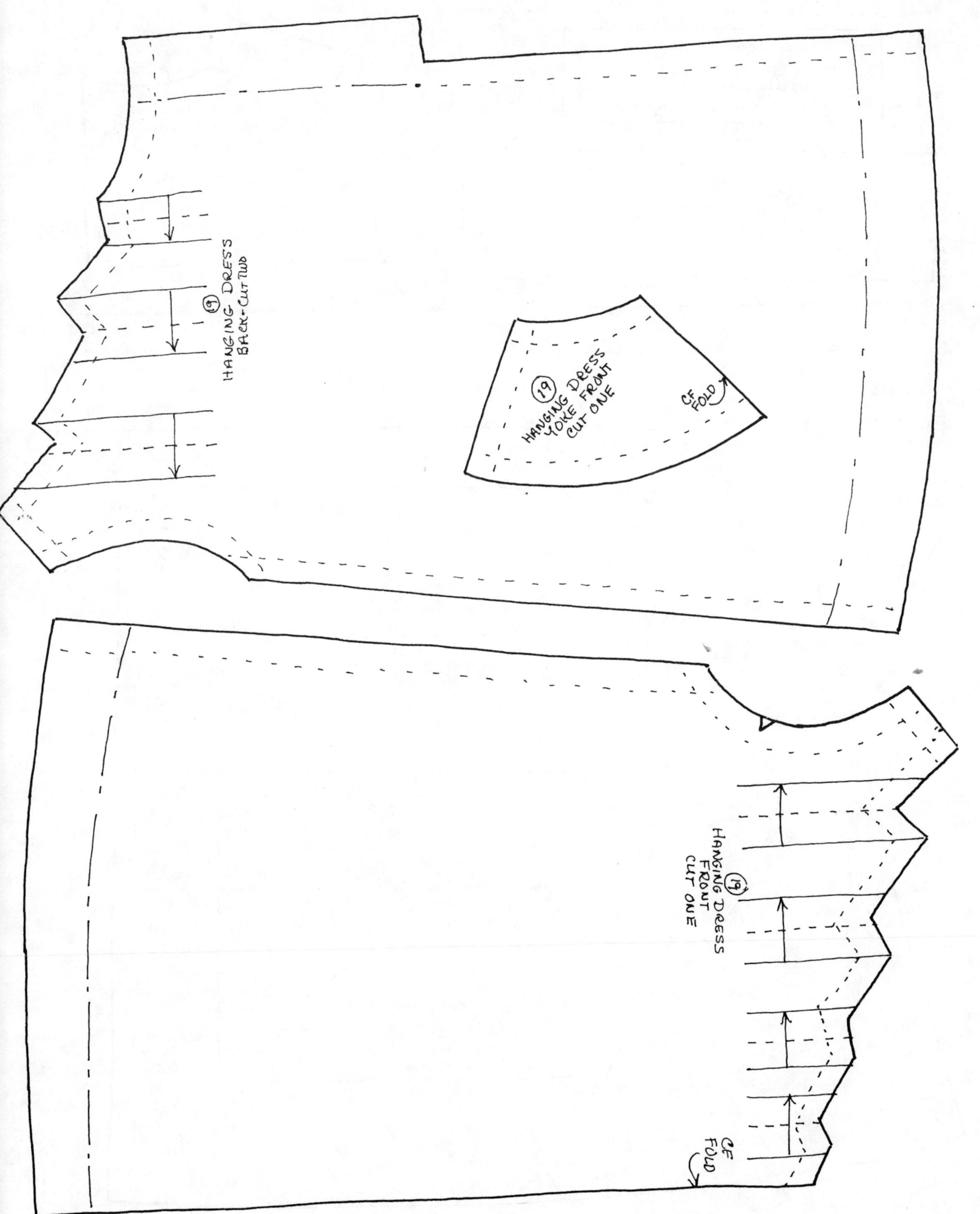
19
HANGING DRESS
BACK-CUT TWO
19
HANGING DRESS
YOKE FRONT
CUT ONE
CF
FOLD
19
HANGING DRESS
FRONT
CUT ONE
CF
FOLD

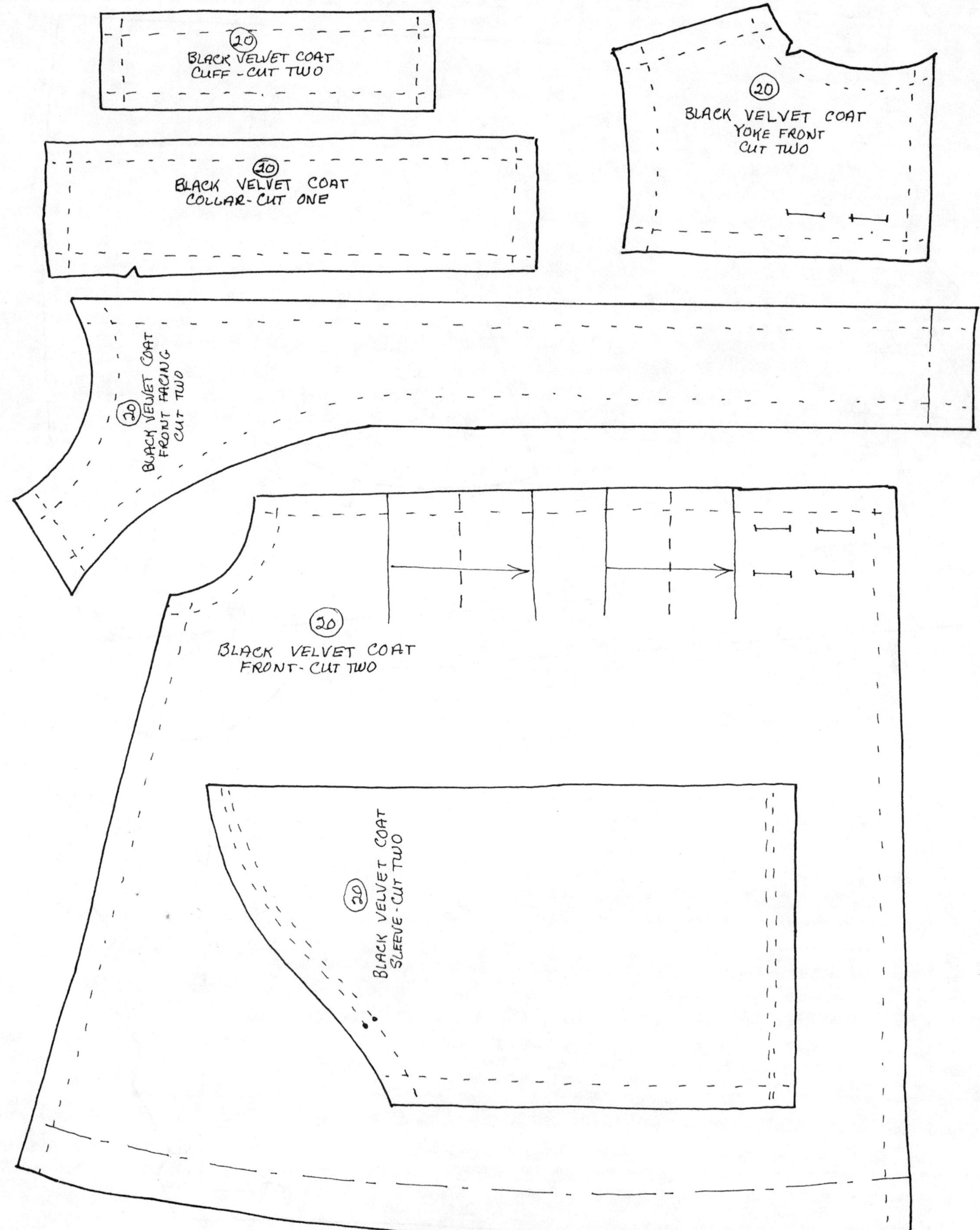
20
BLACK VELVET COAT
CUFF - CUT TWO
20
BLACK VELVET COAT
COLLAR - CUT ONE
20
BLACK VELVET COAT
YOKE FRONT
CUT TWO
20
BLACK VELVET COAT
FRONT FACING
CUT TWO
20
BLACK VELVET COAT
FRONT - CUT TWO
20
BLACK VELVET COAT
SLEEVE - CUT TWO

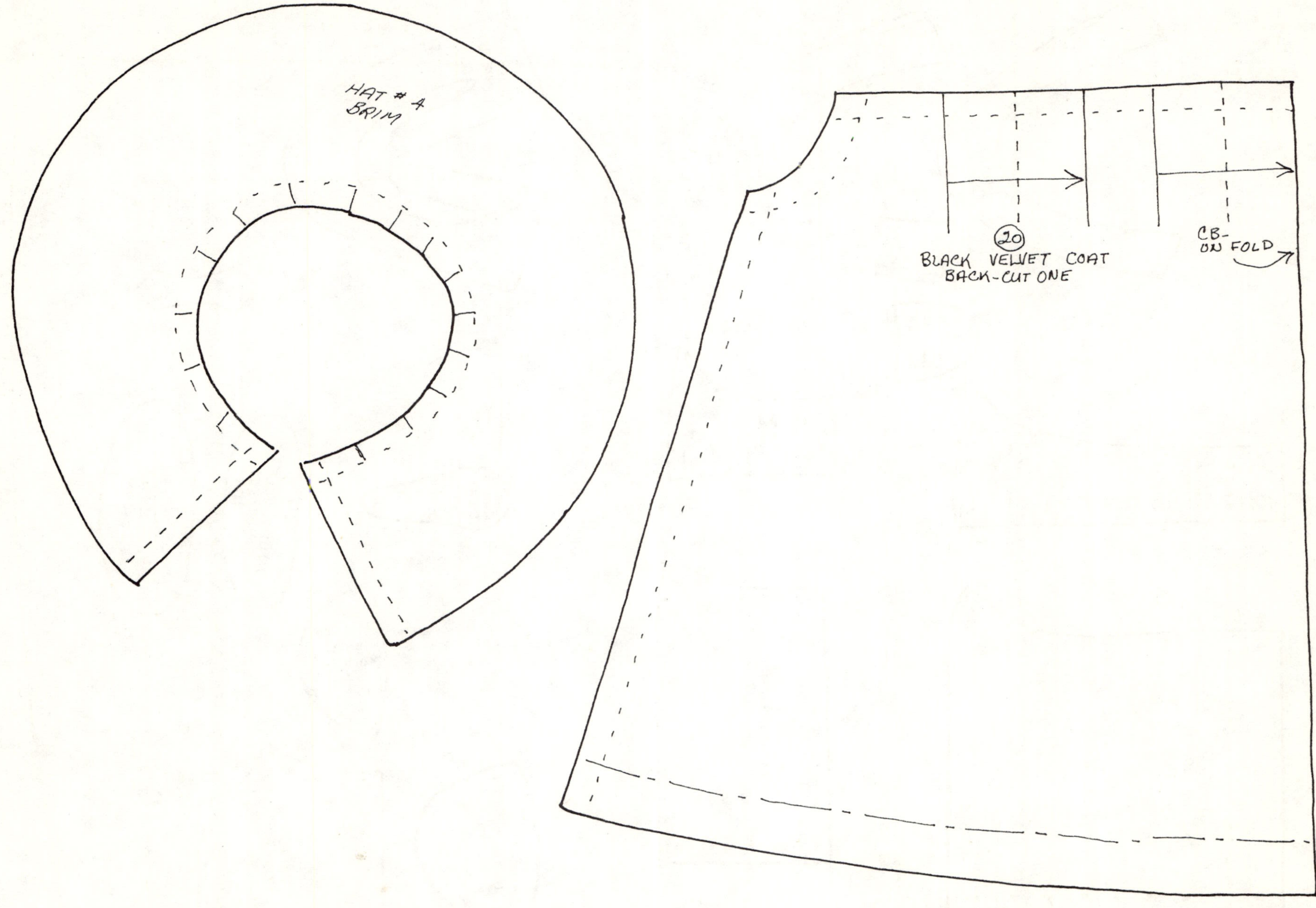
HAT # 4
BRIM
20
BLACK VELVET COAT
BACK-CUT ONE
CB-
ON FOLD

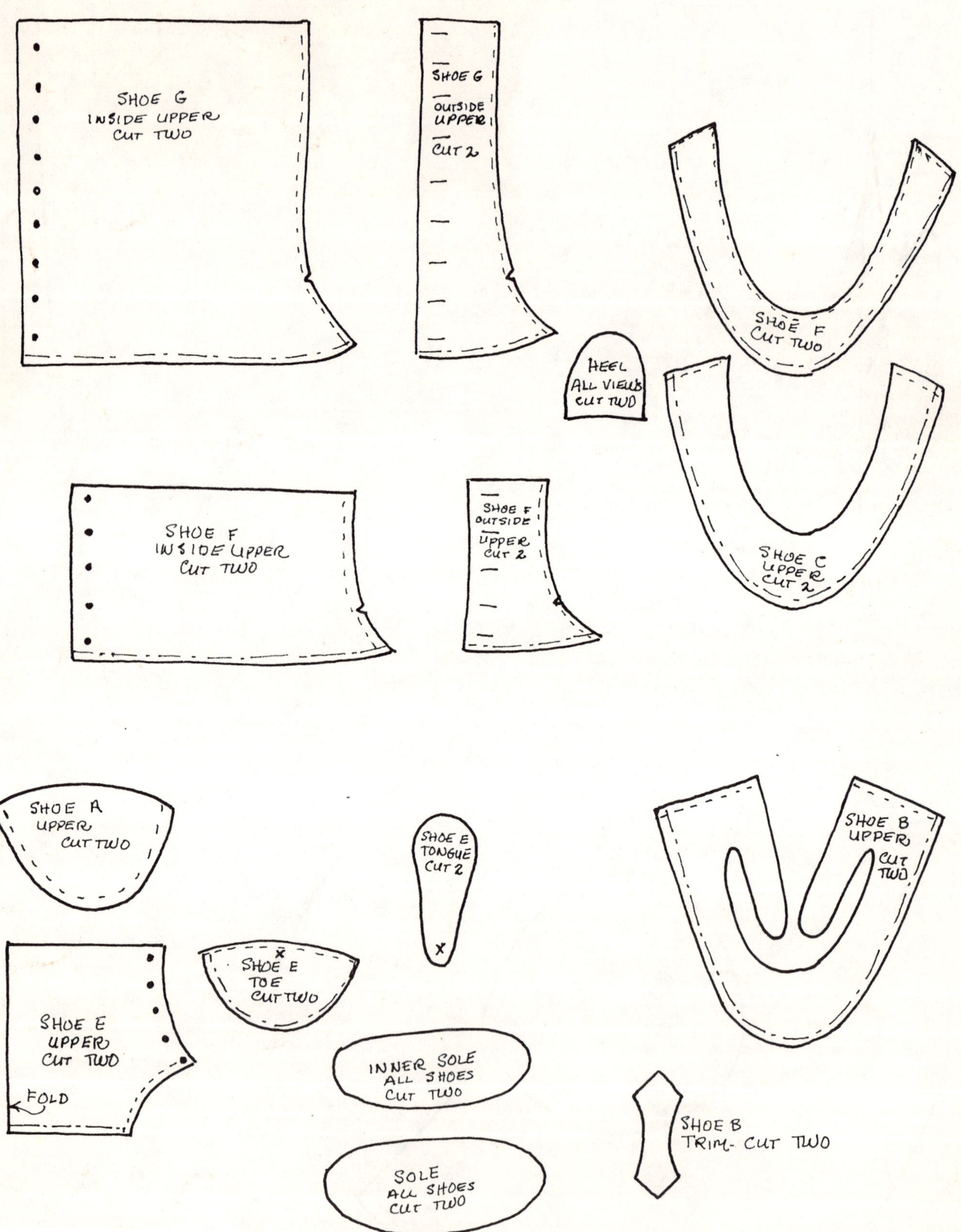
SHOE G
INSIDE UPPER
CUT TWO
SHOE G
OUTSIDE UPPER
CUT 2
SHOE F
CUT TWO
HEEL
ALL VIEWS
CUT TWO
SHOE F
INSIDE UPPER
CUT TWO
SHOE F
OUTSIDE
UPPER
CUT 2
SHOE C
UPPER
CUT 2
SHOE A
UPPER
CUT TWO
SHOE E
TONGUE
CUT 2
SHOE B
UPPER
CUT
TWO
SHOE E
TOE
CUT TWO
SHOE E
UPPER
CUT TWO
FOLD
INNER SOLE
ALL SHOES
CUT TWO
SHOE B
TRIM- CUT TWO
SOLE
ALL SHOES
CUT TWO